African Political, Economic, and Security Issues

Why Real Estate Ownership Security Cannot be Assured via Land Registration in Sub-Saharan Africa

AFRICAN POLITICAL, ECONOMIC, AND SECURITY ISSUES

Additional books in this series can be found on Nova's website under the Series tab.

Additional e-books in this series can be found on Nova's website under the E-book tab.

AFRICAN POLITICAL, ECONOMIC, AND SECURITY ISSUES

WHY REAL ESTATE OWNERSHIP SECURITY CANNOT BE ASSURED VIA LAND REGISTRATION IN SUB-SAHARAN AFRICA

RAYMOND T. ABDULAI
AND
DANIEL DOMEHER

Nova Science Publishers, Inc.
New York

For permission to use material from this book please contact us:
Telephone 631-231-7269; Fax 631-231-8175
Web Site: http://www.novapublishers.com

NOTICE TO THE READER

Additional color graphics may be available in the e-book version of this book.

LIBRARY OF CONGRESS CATALOGING-IN-PUBLICATION DATA

Why real estate ownership security cannot be assured via land registration in sub-Saharan Africa / editors: Raymond T. Abdulai and Daniel Domeher.
p. cm.
Includes index.
ISBN 978-1-61942-668-9 (hardcover)
1. Land titles--Registration and transfer--Africa, Sub-Saharan. 2. Land tenure--Law and legislation--Economic aspects--Africa, Sub-Saharan. 3. Real property--Ownership--Africa, Sub-Saharan. I. Abdulai, Raymond T. II. Domeher, Daniel.
KQC214.W49 2011
333.30967--dc23

2011052250

Published by Nova Science Publishers, Inc. † New York

CONTENTS

PREFACE

It is often argued that land registration is the answer to insecurity of real estate ownership in sub-Saharan Africa and, indeed, the whole of the developing world. This argument is based on the presumption that there is ownership security in the advanced world because every real estate is registered. However, a lot of studies conducted in the developing world have established that ownership security cannot be assured via land registration. This book critically analyses the theoretical principles that underpin land registration systems in order to provide more insights as to why land registration cannot guarantee ownership security. It also examines the nexus between security of ownership and investment.

The study shows that, first of all, the presumption that all advanced nations have 100% land registration systems is mendacious. Secondly, it has been established that land registration plays a very critical role in the economies of countries but it appears that such a role has been completely misunderstood. Primarily, land registration is a record keeping system and the importance of any record keeping system cannot be over-emphasized. The actual purpose that land registration serves is that it creates a real estate ownership database that facilitates real estate transactions like conveyancing, title or ownership searches, and taxation thereby reducing transaction costs. The factors that actually determine ownership security are: (a) societal and legal recognition of ownership; (b) availability of ownership dispute resolution and enforcement institutions; (c) clear demarcation of landed property boundaries; and (d) ownership insurance. In terms of the link between ownership security and investment, the analysis shows that the importance of ownership security has been over hiked - ownership security alone cannot guarantee investment. There are other important drivers of investment and the overarching factor is ability to invest, which is determined mainly by financial capability. Regarding agricultural investment, government prodding in the form of creating an enabling environment, is also a crucial factor.

The policy implications of the findings are as follows. Firstly, governments in sub-Saharan Africa should promote land registration based on the right and critical role it is supposed to play as indicated above. Secondly, the identified determinants of ownership security should inform policy formulation and implementation of programmes aimed at securing ownership. Thirdly, for agricultural investment, particularly, there is the need for government support in the form of a sound socio-economic infrastructural base, investment in storage facilities and agro processing, and direct funding of the agricultural sector via, for example, the provision necessary agricultural implements at subsidised prices. There is also the need for the establishment of specialised financial institutions where they do not exist to provide credit with flexible conditions to serve the peculiar needs of farmers and where such institutions already exist, their activities should focus mainly on channelling credit to the agricultural sector and the operations of the institutions should be devoid of political interferences. Furthermore, international donor community support through the implementation of appropriate programmes that would assist specifically, small-scale farmers is a crucial driver of agricultural investment.

ACKNOWLEDGMENTS

First of all, the authors wish to express their deepest gratitude to Mrs Grace Abdulai and Mrs Esther Domeher, the wives of the first and second authors respectively, the following staff of the School of Built Environment, Liverpool John Moores University: Mr James Hartwell, Dr Wilfred Matipa, Dr Edward Ochieng, and Mr Nazali Mohd Noor as well as Prof Issaka Ndekugri of the School of Technology, Wolverhampton University for their support and encouragement throughout the compilation of this book. Secondly, our special thanks go to the Publishers. Above all our foremost gratitude goes to the Almighty God for bestowing upon us wisdom and understanding and for His guidance and protection throughout the past years.

AUTOBIOGRAPHICAL NOTES

Dr Raymond Talinbe Abdulai is a Senior Lecturer and Head of Research in Real Estate and Planning at the School of the Built Environment, Liverpool John Moores University in the United Kingdom. He holds a PhD, MPhil (Cantab), and a BSc (First Class Honours), all in real estate as well as a PGCertHE. Prior to his appointment at Liverpool JMU, he worked at the School of Technology, Wolverhampton University as a Post-doctoral Research Fellow and Lecturer. He lectured at Kwame Nkrumah University of Science and Technology (KNUST) in Ghana where he also practised as a chartered general practice surveyor before commencing his academic career in the United Kingdom. Raymond's research interests span various facets of real estate including: real estate economics, management, finance, investment, valuation and development; land dispute resolution, especially in the developing world; emerging real estate markets; and landed property rights, particularly, traditional land rights in the developing world.

Raymond has published extensively in reputed journals, conferences, edited books and research monographs, and has three books to his credit. He is currently the Editor-in-Chief of Journal of International Real Estate and Construction Studies (JIRECS), which is indexed in Cabell's Directory of Publishing Opportunities in Economics and Finance. He has served as track and session chair for various international conferences. Raymond also serves on the editorial boards of various international journals. He has won various international awards from Overseas Development Association (ODA), now Department for International Development (DFID), Cambridge University, Royal Institution of Chartered Surveyors (RICS) Education Trust, American and European Real Estate Societies, and Wolverhampton University.

Mr Daniel Domeher is currently a PhD Researcher in property rights registration and access to small and micro-scale enterprises (SMEs) credit and a Visiting Lecturer at the School of the Built Environment, Liverpool John Moores University in the United Kingdom. Daniel holds an MA in Banking and Finance from Sheffield Hallam University in the United Kingdom and a BA degree in Economics and Geography (First Class) from KNUST. Prior to this, he worked as a Management Trainee at Garden City Savings and Loans Ltd. in Kumasi, Ghana. He was at the same time a part-time Lecturer at the School of Business, KNUST. He had also earlier worked at the Department of Economics, KNUST as a Teaching Assistant. Daniel has published in journals and conferences of international repute.

Chapter 1

PROLOGUE

ABSTRACT

This chapter examines various studies on the relationship between land registration on one hand and ownership security, access to formal capital for investment and wealth creation on the other in the developing world. The evidence adduced shows that: (a) land registration per se is incapable of guaranteeing ownership security and, indeed, in some circumstances it can be a source of insecurity; (b) the importance of ownership security in driving investment in land-based activities has been over-emphasised as security alone cannot guarantee investment – there are other very critical factors that drive investment activities; and (c) there is no discernible link between land registration and access to formal credit for investment and development. The real determinants of especially, agricultural investment are identified and discussed. The chapter therefore provides the appropriate context for the discussions that follow in subsequent chapters.

1.1. INTRODUCTION

In sub-Saharan Africa (SSA)[1], traditional/customary systems of real estate[2] ownership operate alongside formal systems, which were introduced

---

[1] SSA by the World Bank designation refers to countries south of the Sahara. They are, therefore, countries that are not part of North Africa (Western Sahara, Morocco, Algeria, Tunisia, Libya and Egypt) but include offshore islands. Details on the countries that constitute SSA together with a map are provided in Section 1. 4.

during the colonial era. The traditional systems are not based on any form of documentation; customarily, proof of ownership is by physical possession and occupation and the recognition of that fact by community members, particularly, adjoining owners (Abdulai, 2010; Antwi, 2000). The longstanding argument that the traditional system of real estate ownership is insecure and that registration of such ownership is the panacea to the problem of insecurity is common knowledge. The argument, which dates back to the colonial era, is premised on the common notion that there is security of real estate ownership in the advanced world because all real estate ownership is registered in every developed country.

Extending the argument that equates land registration to ownership security, it is asserted that land registration provides a secure form of collateral for mortgage purposes and thus guarantees access to formal capital for investment, wealth creation, poverty reduction, and development (Mahama, 2008; Derban et al., 2002; de Soto, 2000). Therefore, supported by the international donor community, land registration policies have been religiously pursued since the colonial era up to the present time, supposedly, to establish ownership security. The support is manifested by the huge expenses incurred in pursuing and implementing land registration policies and programmes respectively in the developing world. Such expenses, for example, range from US$ 20.51 million in Ghana, US$ 27 million in Malawi, US$ 106 million in Bolivia, US$ 140 million in the Dominican Republic to US$ 195 million in Ukraine (Griffith-Charles, 2004). This has triggered various studies to be conducted on the real impact of land registration on ownership security and for that matter access to formal credit, investment, wealth creation and development.

There is overwhelming evidence (as will be established later in the literature), which bespeaks that there is no discernible link between land registration on one hand and ownership security, access to formal credit, investment, poverty reduction and development on the other. The overall aim of this book is to provide a theoretical explanation as to why the evidence from various studies conducted in many countries shows that real estate ownership security and the occurrence of the other above mentioned variables cannot be assured via land registration. The aim is pursued by discussing the theoretical principles that underpin the forms of land registration systems, which exist globally and their practical application.

[2] Real estate is a term that connotes land and/or the developments on it. The other terminology for it is real property or landed property. This is explained in more detail in chapter two.

The object of this chapter is to set the necessary scene for the rest of the book. To intimate what follows, section two reviews the studies on the nexus between land registration and real estate ownership security. Following on, section three assesses the impact of ownership security on investment; the relationship between land registration and access to formal capital for investment is also examined in this section. Section four concentrates on the drivers of investment whilst the penultimate section provides details of the countries that constitute SSA. The chapter is concluded in section six.

1.2. Land Registration and Landed Property Ownership Security

The importance of landed property cannot be over-emphasised in any economy. Land, for example, is a primary commodity that provides space for various activities. It is the most basic and vital aspect of subsistence for many people around the world and therefore a strategic socio-economic asset, particularly in poor societies where wealth and survival are measured by control of, and access to land (Lund, 2010; USAID, 2005; Deininger, 2003). In many developing countries, land accounts for 50% to 75% of national wealth (Bell, 2006). Landed property is, for that reason, far too important a subject to be left out of consideration in any serious macroeconomic deliberation and in the collective quest for sustainable development, poverty alleviation, human rights and access to justice.

Due to the important role that landed property plays in the economies of nations, landed property ownership insecurity is a major concern to both developed and developing countries as well as the international donor community. Indeed, the quest for secure ownership[3] dates back to several centuries ago. Feder and Nishio (1999) referring to the books of Genesis 23 and Jeremiah 32 in the Holy Bible explains how Abraham and the prophet Jeremiah sought for secure ownership of different parcels of land some 4,000 years ago. Prospective investors may not invest in landed property related activities unless they are confident that their ownership would be secure (Abdulai and Hammond, 2010). Security of ownership is thus considered as

[3] Landed property ownership security will be considered later in the book where it will be explained in detail but it will suffice here to define ownership security as the degree of certainty that a person's rights to landed property will be recognized by law and, especially, by members of the society and protected when there are challenges to such rights (Abdulai, 2010; Abdulai et al., 2007; FAO, 2005).

one of the factors than can establish a structure of economic incentives for investing in landed property related activities (Deininger, 2003; Quan, 2000).

Admittedly, there is an assertion that ownership insecurity is equally an incentive to invest. In this regard, Sjaastad and Bromley (1997), for example, argue that investments in trees, irrigation furrows, buildings or other fixed structures may provide a litigant in a land dispute with an unassailable case and that even though insecurity is a disincentive to invest, it is paradoxically often also an incentive to invest for security. This argument implicitly assumes that the state sponsored legal framework guarantees: (a) the protection of investors in landed property related activities whether or not they truly own the property; and (b) payment of compensation to investors who eventually lose their investment in landed property related activities whether or not they truly own the property.

However, undertaking visible investments on land, for example, may demonstrate an individual's presence or occupation of the land, which associates the investor with the land but this association, cannot be equated to recognition as the rightful owner by the community members and the legal system. In fact, investing in a parcel of land that one does not rightfully own will in itself trigger disputes or insecurity rather than reduce or eliminate the disputes. Indeed, when an ownership dispute arises on a parcel of land and it is brought to the state sponsored courts for resolution, what has to be established by the courts beyond reasonable doubt is the true owner of the land (Abdulai, 2010; Abdulai et al., 2007). Court judgements are thus not delivered based on whether the land has already been developed by any of the disputants or whether any of the disputants has invested in the land. Investments per se cannot therefore provide the investor with indefeasible landed property rights.

There are various negative ramifications of landed property ownership insecurity. Firstly, insecurity of ownership in the form of land disputes negatively affects infrastructure and real estate development projects and agricultural activities. When a dispute arises over a plot of land where a real estate development project is to be carried out, the development cannot proceed until the land dispute is effectively settled. This constitutes a source of major risks to investors. In terms of agricultural activities, a study from Uganda established that land disputes reduced the output on a plot of land by at least 30% (Deininger and Castagnini, 2002). The negative impact is even more pronounced where there are delays in settling the land dispute in the state sponsored courts. Such protracted litigation often stifles land-based economic activities including construction or real estate development projects as court injunctions are issued against any use of the land until the cases are decided by the courts. Secondly, in a climate of insecure landed property ownership, entrepreneurs are often compelled to spend valuable resources defending their landed property rights, thereby, diverting effort and such resources meant for other productive purposes like investment (Deininger, 2003).

Thirdly, there is a direct link between land disputes and civil strife. In explaining the causes of civil strife, traditional models do not consider the role of land disputes and rather focus on rent-seeking arguments (Collier and Hoeffler, 1998). However, although not all wars are caused by land disputes, since the beginning of recorded history, disputes over land have often led to some of the most damaging forms of civil strife, including large-scale wars. Indeed, population growth, globalization and environmental stresses have tended to exacerbate many people's perception of land as an essential but dwindling resource, thereby strengthening and tightening the connection between land disputes and violent conflict (USAID, 2005).

Civil strife arising from land disputes, with devastating human and economic consequences, has been reported in many developing countries like: Uganda, Angola, Tajikistan, Kyrgyzstan, Uzbekistan, Kazakhstan, Namibia, Papua New Guinea, Peru, Brazil, East Timor, Kosovo, Mozambique, Mexico, Iraq, Nigeria, Ethiopia, Nepal and Venezuela (USAID, 2005); Zimbabwe, Guatemala, Columbia and El Salvador (Deininger, 2003); Democratic Republic of Congo (Huggins et al., 2005); India (Conroy et al., 1998); Nicaragua (Powelson and Stock, 1990); Kenya (Lumumba, 2004; Okoth-Ogendo, 1996); Somalia (Farah, 2004); Sierra Leone (Richard, 2003); South Africa (Bullard and Waters, 1996); and Ghana (Abdulai, 2010; Abdulai et al. 2007). Land disputes also provide fodder for conflict entrepreneurs who use them to manipulate the emotional, cultural and symbolic dimensions of land for personal political or material gain, thereby fomenting civil strife as in the cases of Rwanda and Burundi (USAID, 2005; Andre and Platteau, 1998). It is self-evident in war-torn countries in the developing world that civil strife normally reverses the clock of progress or development as many people are displaced and impoverished, human resources are lost via deaths, children are orphaned, a country's infrastructural base is destroyed and property worth billions of US$ destroyed.

The link between insecurity of landed property ownership and development has not also been lost to the international development agencies. The World Bank, for example, has identified landed property ownership insecurity in the form of land disputes together with poor governance as a major factor inhibiting development in many African countries (World Bank, 2007) whilst landed property ownership security has been identified by UN-

HABITAT as one of the most important catalysts in stabilizing communities, improving shelter conditions, reducing social exclusion and improving access to urban services (UNCHS, 1999). The Millennium Development Goals also give prominence to the role of secure land rights in helping to alleviate poverty and achieve development in third world countries (Payne et al. 2007).

Thc importance of landed property ownership security and the negative impacts of ownership insecurity have triggered a search for systems that would establish security. Land registration has been embraced as the answer to ownership insecurity in sub-Saharan Africa and the developing world as a whole and it is premised on the common notion that there is security of real estate ownership in the advanced world because every developed country has a comprehensive land registration system. Thus, efforts at securing landed property rights have often concentrated on the formulation and implementation of land registration policies and programmes respectively.

However, albeit land registration is has been equated to ownership security, empirical evidence from various studies conducted in countries like Afghanistan (World Bank, 2006), Cambodia and Rwanda (Durand-Lasserve and Payne, 2006), Philippines and Honduras (World Bank, 2005a), Egypt (Sims, 2002), Ghana (Abdulai, 2010; Abdulai et al., 2007; Agbosu, 1990; Woodman, 1986), Kenya (McAuslan, 2000; Migot-Adholla et al., 1994), Uganda (McAuslan, 2000; West, 2000), Ivory Coast (Stamm, 2000), India (Banerjee, 2002; Sukumaran, 1999), and Pacific Islands (Acquaye, 1984) has shown that real estate ownership security cannot be assured via land registration. The same evidence has been established by the studies of Payne et al. (2009), Bromley (2008), Toulmin (2006), Fitzpatrick (2005), de Janvry et al. (2001) and Barrows and Roth (1990).

Indeed, in the developed world, there is evidence from case law that shows that genuine owners of registered landed property have lost their landed property through civil litigation. In the American case of *Eliason v. Wilborn* (1929), Mr and Mrs Eliason of Cook County in Illinois owned a parcel of land registered under a Torrens Act. They entrusted their certificate of title to a prospective purchaser who used it to forge a transfer to himself, registered it and proceeded to sell the property to a man named Wilborn. After extended litigation, which ended in the Supreme Court of the United States, the defrauded proprietors failed to recover the land. They then filed a claim of losses from the state but were advised that they must secure a judgment before they could be paid. They had already been in the courts for several years and were, as their attorneys expressed it, "so fed up with litigation that they decided to pocket their losses". Other cases with such evidence include

Attorney-General v. Odell (1906) 2 Ch 47 (English case), *Gibbs v. Meyser* [1891] A.C. 248 (Australian case), *Gill v. Frances Co* (1937) (American case) and *Frazer v. Walker* [1967] 1 A.C. 569 (New Zealand case).

It is, therefore, not surprising that Payne et al. (2007) have done a critical analysis of various studies that have supposedly linked land registration to ownership security in the developing world and conclude that the residents in those studies already enjoyed ownership security before the introduction of land registration programmes. According to Okoin (1999) in Ivory Coast, although reports of land registration under the Rural Land Plan in some parts showed that open landed property disputes or conflicts were non-existent when the property was being registered, it was because outstanding disputes had been dealt with by informal dispute resolution institutions prior to the land registration team's arrival. It implies that the informal dispute resolution institutions had been able to resolve any disputes or conflicts before registration and the lack of open disputes was not due to land registration.

Abdulai (2010) has concluded in his research that studies that have supposedly linked land registration to ownership security either have research methodological problems or what constitutes ownership security appears to have been misinterpreted. In unauthorised settlements, empirical evidence from studies conducted in Mexico (Angel et al., 2006), Tanzania (Kironde, 2006), South Africa (Allanic, 2003) and Peru (Ramirez et al., 2005; Kagawa and Turkstra, 2002) has also shown that residents in such settlements already enjoyed de facto ownership security before the introduction of land registration programmes and therefore ownership security did not emanate from land registration.

It has been established by other studies that land registration can even be a source of insecurity in some circumstances. According to Durand-Lasserve and Payne (2006) land registration can disadvantage poor people who lose the security provided by the traditional systems of landed property ownership whilst being unable to complete the bureaucratic process of land registration - in worst cases it has created opportunities for the powerful in society to override traditional systems of ownership, thereby, displacing vulnerable owners. Re-echoing this point, Deininger (2003), Deininger and Feder (2001) and Janvry et al. (2001) note that land registration is not always necessary or sufficient for high level of ownership security and that in most cases it creates new sources of conflicts if formal landed property rights are assigned without due recognition of traditional arrangements.

Migot-Adholla et al. (1994), Green (1987), Bruce (1986) and Okoth-Ogendo (1982) have highlighted the negative and startling impacts of land registration in Kenya. These include: (a) heightened inequalities in landownership and agricultural incomes, leading to increased landlessness via land sales and growing rural-urban migration; (b) diminished food security and increased vulnerability to drought amongst groups whose access to land had been diminished by land registration; and (c) increased level of land disputes. In Rwanda and Zimbabwe, land registration created more land disputes and uncertainty as well as denied land access to the poor and other marginalised groups like women whose rights were well protected under the customary systems of landownership (Plateau, 1996).

1.3. Impact of Landed Property Ownership Security on Investment

The theoretical model linking ownership security to especially, agricultural investment has been explained by Roth and Haase (1998) and Feder et al. (1986), which is summarised as follows. Ownership security is perceived to promote investment through two main channels, which are the demand-side and supply-side channels.

The demand-side effects deal effectively with the incentives that security provides farmers to invest in land related activities. It postulates that higher levels of ownership security increase the demand for investment by farmers. The rise in investment will then increase the yield per acre and hopefully bring more income into the pockets of the farmers. Farmers are said to demand for more investment with improved ownership security because of two principal reasons. The first reason is the fact that enhanced ownership security makes it more possible for farmers to reap the fruits of their investment. The second reason relates to the fact that enhanced ownership security reduces landownership disputes allowing farmers more productive time and resources, which would otherwise have been spent on defending their rights to land through civil litigation and other means.

On the supply-side, ownership security is said to influence investment through the provision of incentives to the banks to provide farmers with funds for investment. Security is thus believed to guarantee the supply of credit for investment via the use of land as collateral since the ownership of the land is considered as secure. It is further asserted that security facilitates transactions in land markets, raises land values and enhances the credit worthiness of farmers by improving upon the value of the land used as collateral. In other words, security makes land an acceptable collateral asset by financial institutions thereby guaranteeing access to formal credit by farmers. The supply-side effect is particularly relevant where the demand-side effects have been weakened by the lack of internal funds on the part of the farmers. A diagrammatic representation of this security-investment model is presented in Figure 1.1.

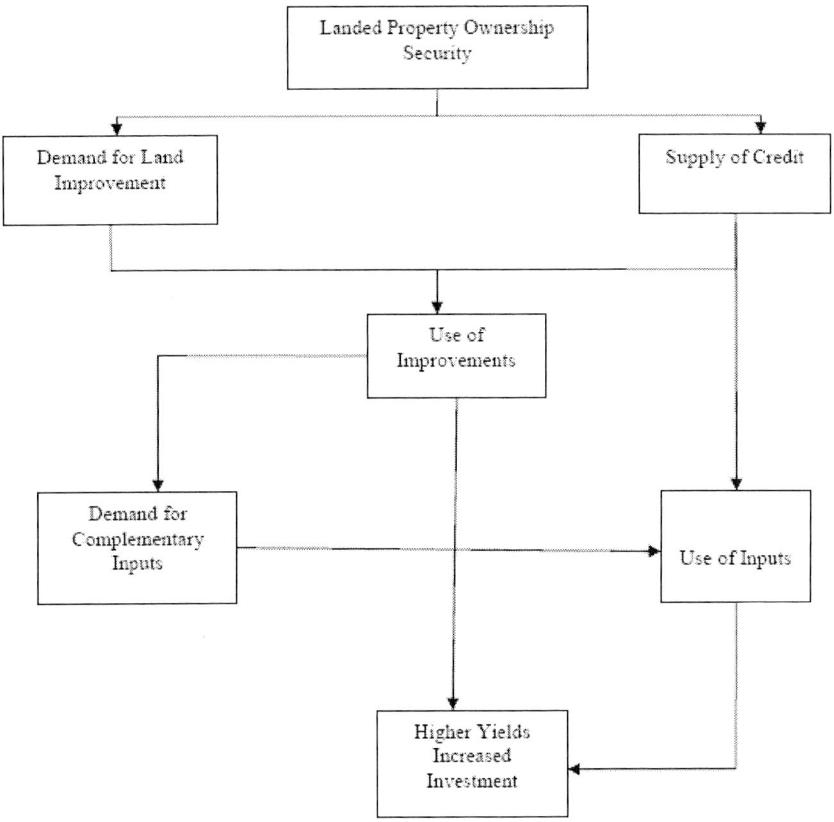

Source: Roth and Haase (1998).

Figure 1.1. Security-Investment Model.

The model presents ownership security as if it definitely guarantees agricultural investment across time and space. However, according to Brasselle et al. (2001) there is a methodological problem with the studies that tend to conclude that security guarantees agricultural investments as they fail to appropriately control for the endogenous element embedded in the positive relationship that exist between security and investments. Studies that have dealt appropriately with this element of endogeneity are said to usually end up with conclusions which are directly opposite the conclusions of studies failing to control for endogeneity. Plateau (1996) re-echoes this in his argument that any observed positive relationship between security and investment should not be taken to mean that the two are automatically causally linked. He argues that security and investment simply have a positive relation (they move in the same direction) but, however, notes that if two variables are positively related, it does not necessarily mean they are causally linked.

A study by Migot-Adholla et al. (1991), for example, found that about 78% of secure landholders had undertaken investments in land improvement activities as against 26% of insecure landholders. However, just like other studies, this study, failed to match the socio-economic profiles of the two groups of respondents (those with secure ownership and those with insecure ownership) with their observed investment activities. It is possible that those with secure ownership coincidentally could, for instance, have higher income levels or other sources of income and that is why they are observed to have better access to credit and undertake more investments than the other group of respondents. A simple cross tabulation of the income levels or sources of income of respondents with observed investments could bring out other important but often ignored determinants of such investments.

The demand-side effects as postulated by the above model appear to have some inherent weakness that will not permit the realisation of the claimed investment and an increase in productivity. The model fails to specify the degree of security required to achieve the investment and productivity outcomes it predicts. It is possible to have different levels of security associated with various kinds of investments given the fact that security has different dimensions and degrees as will be established later. Demand is an economic concept that involves two key elements - willingness and ability. Investment demand must thus involve both the willingness and ability to invest. A farmer may have his or her ownership secure but may not be willing or capable of investing in land to improve upon yield and income levels. Willingness and ability go together such that the absence of one has the potential to hinder any investment activity. Willingness without ability to invest is nothing but a mere wish; such empty wishes, however, do not create investments but rather wishes that need to be backed by ability to invest for investment to happen. This implies that effective demand for investment activities is a very critical determinant. Ownership security may only provide an incentive to invest, which means that to some extent, it only influences the motivation, desire or willingness to invest but this cannot be equated to effective demand for investment activities. Furthermore, there are other factors like expected investment returns and the existence of an enabling investment environment.

If the model is anything to go by, the demand-side effects are only realisable under the assumption that farmers have the financial and other resources to undertake investments and that the appropriate investment environment exists. An enabling investment environment should be seen as one that reduces risks and enhances the prospects of investments. This will include an environment where there is availability of irrigation and storage facilities, good transport network and easy access to markets. Adams et al. (1999) agree with this by their assertion that securing ownership within an environment full of various constraint factors will not bring about the desired effects in terms of investment. Unfortunately, these desirable conditions do not exist in Africa (Platteau, 1996). The absence of this enabling environment is one of the biggest constraints of agricultural productivity in the continent. Thus the argument linking ownership security to investment in a manner to suggest that secure landownership will automatically lead to increase demand for investment in agricultural production is unsustainable in an environment where these agricultural investment enhancing conditions are non-existent.

Efforts at promoting agricultural investments seem to have ignored these very important factors and over concentrated on securing landownership. Admittedly, security of ownership is required for investment in land related activities but that alone cannot guarantee investment by farmers as the above model portrays. Thus, to promote agricultural investments, the focus should not be on securing landownership alone. There are other important factors that need to be given serious consideration. In the unlikely event where farmers (with secure landownership) are financially capable of investing, the absence of the above desirable conditions for agricultural investment will increase the cost and risk of investment, which together will work to reduce willingness to invest and hence reduce the actual demand for investment.

Apart from the lack of willingness to invest in agricultural activities, due to the poor conditions already mentioned, ownership security may also fail to yield the required demand-side effects because of the high poverty levels in Africa. According to Draman (2003), out of the 25 poorest countries in the world, 11 are found in West Africa. About 75% of Africa's poor people reside in the rural areas (McCord et al., 2005) who are mainly engaged in agriculture for survival. Twenty-percent of the world's population representing 1.2 billion people in 2003 lived on less than US$ 1 per day; 70% of these were rural dwellers and 90% were in Asia and sub-Saharan Africa (Thirtle et al., 2003) - these statistics have not changed significantly since then. It is therefore not astounding that the World Bank's research shows that Africa is a critical development priority since it has some of the world's poorest countries and during the past two decades, the number of poor people in the region has doubled to 300 million, which is more than 40% of the region's total population (World Bank, 2007). These figures point to the fact that farmers in Africa are financially incapable of undertaking various investments on their farms. It implies that even if the landownership of farmers is secure, it will not guarantee an increase in demand for agricultural investments.

Where the demand-side fails to produce the expected effects due to some of the weaknesses identified above, the security-investment model further postulates that security can induce investment through a different channel – the supply-side as explained supra. Wannasai and Shrestha (2007), however, explain that the supply side argument is not applicable to all farmers as some limiting factors may undermine agricultural profitability, which will make it difficult for some farmers to access formal credit. In a rain-fed agricultural regime (which is generally the case in Africa) where the necessary agro-infrastructural base is weak, where inputs are difficult to access, and where ready markets for agricultural products are not there, agricultural investment will remain unprofitable and unattractive. The banks may therefore not be willing to fund such unprofitable investments and the farmers themselves are likely to divert any funds made available to them into financing their consumption expenditures instead of investing. The same factors that limit the realisation of the demand-side effects as discussed above may also hinder the realisation of the supply-side effects.

There may be several factors that contribute to the high level of risks associated with the agricultural sector, which make the sector unattractive to private commercial banks. However, the overarching factor is explained by the cobweb theory in economic literature. The theory was propounded by Nicholas Kaldor in 1934. It explains the continuous or repetitive fluctuations in the price and output of agricultural products. This theory is only applicable where the following conditions exist: (a) production must respond to price changes in a perfectly competitive market where an individual's production plans will not affect the market and it is assumed that current prices will persist into the future (this allows plans for future production to be determined by the present price level); (b) there must be a time lag between price change and production – that is, it should take some considerable period for production to respond to price changes; and finally (c) supply availability sets the prices and it is not applicable in monopolistic situations.

If prices are high today and farmers expect that these prices will remain high in the future, they will tend to expand production to increase supply in the future. However, if prices are low today and are expected to remain so in the future, farmers are likely to reduce production now and hence will supply in the future. The cobweb theorem is diagrammatically illustrated in Figure 1.2 below.

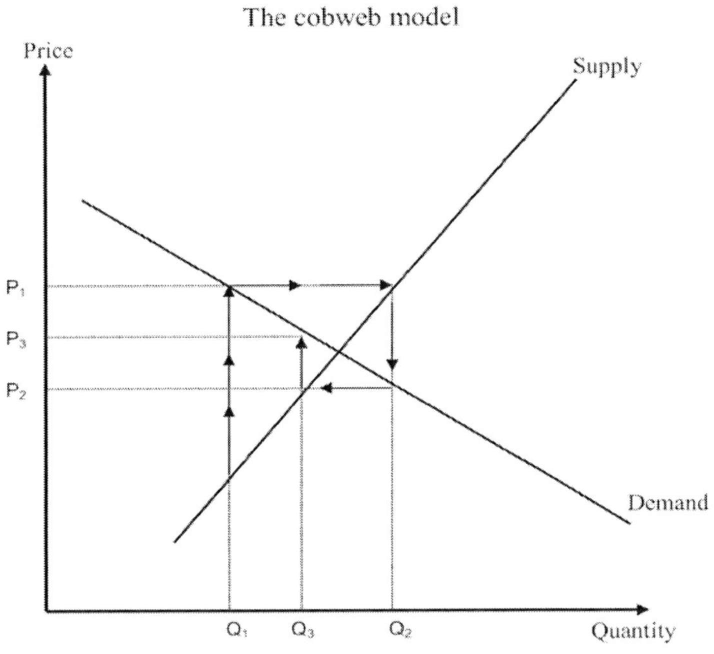

Figure 1.2. Cobweb Model.

The point where the demand and supply curves intersect is the equilibrium point and demand is equal to supply at that point. Assume three time periods T_1, T_2 and T_3 where T_1 is the current time period, T_2 is the future time period after T_1 and T_3 the future time period after T_2. Where for example farmers experience low harvest in any particular period, say, T_1, this will move supply to Q_1. At Q_1, demand will exceed supply creating a shortage in the market, which will in turn put upward pressure on the price to rise to P_1. If farmers then expect that P_1 will persist, they will plan to increase their supply to Q_2 at T_2. However, this large increase in supply as shown in the diagram creates a surplus in the market and farmers cannot sell all their stock unless they accept lower prices. This will exert downward pressure on the price to fall eventually to P_2. This cycle repeats itself with fluctuations between very high prices and low supply (P_1 Q_1) on one hand and very low prices and high supply (P_2, Q_2) on the other hand.

It appears that the problem faced by the poor rural farmers in Africa is attributable to this phenomenon. During periods of good harvest, in an environment where there are no storage facilities and ready markets, prices fall so low and farmers are faced with the option of accepting very low prices for their products or allow these products to go rotten. These prices are usually not high enough to enable them recoup their investments. Those farmers who would have financed their production with formal credit will find it difficult to repay the loans and may never go in for anymore loans even where it is readily available.

Periods of favourably high prices, however, are associated with a considerable reduction in supply as shown in Figure 1.2 above. Under circumstances like these the farmer loses, whether the price level is favourable or not. These fluctuations could be quite considerable as can be seen from the diagram. This makes it difficult to predict farmers' revenue with a reasonable degree of confidence, which makes farmers revenue unreliable. Thus it seems that this cobweb phenomenon is responsible for the highly risky, unprofitable and unattractive nature of agriculture to formal lenders in Africa. Without any deliberate comprehensive intervention by government, this price-output spiral will continue and the rising poverty amongst farmers may never come to halt.

Some commentators including Deininger and Chamorrow (2002) have also attributed the credit constraint faced by farmers to the absence of functioning credit markets. It should be noted, however, that the problem of farmers in Africa is not so much about the non-existence of functional credit markets. An efficient and functional credit market will ensure that only the credit worthy borrowers get financial support. In that case most farmers in Africa will still be faced with credit constraints even if such credit markets exist given the kind of challenges that exist in the agricultural sector.

Furthermore, proponents of the security-investment model maintain that where farmers with personal financial constraints are unable to access formal credit, security could still enhance investments in that, it is capable of promoting active land market activities, which would permit the transfer of land from such ineffective and incapable land owners to those who are able to invest (Feder and Nishio, 1999). However, de Souza (2000) aptly notes that insecurity does not necessarily hinder active land market transactions.

It is important to note that ownership security only plays a facilitating role in land market activities by reducing or eliminating any doubts regarding true ownership, which then enhances the speed of any given land transaction as well as reduces transactions costs. The vibrant land markets that security is purported to enhance may not exist in rural Africa where most of the agrarian population reside and security of landownership per se will not be able to promote the development of such markets. This is as a result of the "deprived and unattractive" nature of these areas for both residential and commercial purposes. For example, according to the World Bank (2010) rural population across the developing world has lower rates of infrastructure access than urban population - 65% of urban households in low-income countries have access to electricity, but only 17% of rural households do. With the consequent low demand for rural lands, the abundant supply of secure land will not increase market activity to any significant level. This will rather depress rural land values by margins that will render land unacceptable as a collateral asset by banks.

Even if farmers' ownership of land is secure, which they want to use as collateral, they are still unlikely to catch the attention of private commercial banks due to the following reasons. The first reason is that, if all the banks begin to advance credit to farmers based on the acceptance of collateral, the unprofitable nature of agriculture as explained above will definitely cause farmers to default since they most often do not have other sources of income. Mortgagees are likely to foreclose the mortgages by attempting to sell the land used as collateral. This response will in itself exacerbate their plight by causing prices of the properties to fall sharply as supply will tend to exceed demand. Secondly, secure land in remote or rural areas will fail to attract banks as the realisation of such land may be difficult by virtue of their location.

Also, assuming that banks accept secure land as collateral on the basis of which they advance credit, the poor rural farmers who need credit the most will not benefit even with secure land rights because of the nature, location and hence the value of land they possess. Carter et al. (1997) argue that biases usually exist in the credit market in favour of the more affluent large-scale farmers to the disadvantage of the poor majority small-scale farmers. Atwood (1990) therefore asserts that securing the landownership of as many farmers as possible will not in many situations, especially in Africa guarantee an increase in the number of potential borrowers.

Generally, farmers may undertake some investments under some amount of perceived insecurity. In the presence of insecurity, such farmers may eventually be evicted which means they will lose their livelihood. However, if their perception of insecurity does not materialise and no evictions occur, they will not lose their investment. For example, Wannasai and Shrestha (2007) pointed out in their study that: (a) about 67% of farmers were found to continue to invest in long-term crops irrespective of whether or not the level of security they experienced had changed; (b) some residents whose land rights were considered insecure were also found to be investing in long-term crops; and (c) both secure and unsecure farmers allocated more than 80% of their land to long-term crop production.

The above indicates that at least not all people are so much bothered about security issues in taking investment decisions. Farmers at any point in time could be expected to invest to meet their needs under a given budget constraint and at any level of insecurity or risk, they will not starve because of insecurity. Life is all about risk taking and it should be recognised that people usually do not fear taking risk if the benefit is expected to be crucial and substantial for their survival. Since people appear to be willing to invest with some level of risk or insecurity, what is important is to identify the probability of eviction at which they will not invest at all. Risk or insecurity of landed property ownership may not prevent farmers from investing but inability certainly will. Need and ability are thus critical driving forces of investment activities.

Some commentators, writing on the link between security and agricultural investment tend to contradict themselves. For instance, Pingali (1989) attributes the absence of investment in intensive agricultural activities to the lack ownership security under traditional systems, which he describes as communal. He recognises that under the said communal system, individuals obtain the right to only cultivate a piece of land and such rights are lost once the individuals abandon the land to fallow. During the fallow period, the land is said to return to the communal pool and anybody can use it. However, the author acknowledges that even under this communal system one can maintain his right to the land as long as it is occupied and cultivated. From his own argument, it implies that there is security under the communal landownership system. Thus the practice of shifting cultivation (which implies lack of agricultural intensification) cannot be attributed to landownership insecurity. If farmers are capable of undertaking intensive agricultural activities as well as improving soil fertility artificially, they will do that to avoid the inconvenience of moving from one parcel of land to another since their continuous cultivation of the land takes away any threat of losing their rights. Therefore the absence of intensification is a reflection of farmers' incapability to invest in improving the soil fertility and not as a result of landownership insecurity.

Wannasai and Shrestha (2007) observe a reduction in the production of annual or short term crops in favour of investments in perennial or long term crops in their study area and attribute this investment behaviour to an improvement in security. According to price theory, however, producers will only produce a good if consumers are willing and able to pay a price high enough to make its production profitable (Lipsey, 1999). Therefore, if the production of perennial crops is unprofitable, farmers will not invest in them even when their rights to the land are secure. With the right conditions and granted that an investment will be profitable, farmers whether with or without secure land rights will be willing to undertake any kind of investments if they are financially capable contrary to the argument that security guarantees investment.

Another contradictory and flawed argument that links security to investment is advanced by Feder and Onchan (1987) who claimed to have conducted a study that established the necessary evidence in South East Asia. According to the authors, the purpose of their study was two-fold: (a) to confirm empirically that landownership security induces higher farm investment and land improvements; and (b) to estimate the magnitude of such effects. Feder and Onchan (1987, p.312) observe in their study as follows:

> Legislation formalising land ownership was first introduced in the second half of the nineteenth century and several successive legislation addressed aspects of legal ownership. The comprehensive Land Code of 1954 ....identified two types of secure documents: N.S.-4 and N.S.-3 or N.S.-3K. These documents contain a demarcation of land boundaries and allow the owner to sell, transfer and legally mortgage the land. While N.S.-4 is a full or registered title deed, the N.S.-3 documents ("certificates of utilisation") serve almost the same function......the banks will lend equally, irrespective of whether the land has a title or a certificate of utilization (Williamson, 1983, p.10). Because full title deeds are rare in our study areas, the N.S.-3 and N.S.-3K documents are classified as "titled land" for our purposes here.
>
> About half of Thailand's area is classified as forest reserve land; it belongs to the state. However, about a quarter of this land is actually under cultivation by squatters who occupy it illegally.....Irrespective of the length of the de facto possession, squatters on public forest lands cannot obtain titles or certificates of utilization.....Because these areas often are adjacent to legally held private lands, the situation in Thailand is well suited to study the link between ownership security and investment using cross-sectional farm-level data....About 200 farmers were interviewed in each province and the sample was split between residents of forest reserve areas (squatters) and legal owners.

> Squatters on public lands lack security of ownership and are subject to possible eviction. However, eviction is infrequent in Thailand because of social and political constraints. Data from the study area indicate a relatively low lifetime eviction probability of 7.5% for squatters. It is still higher than the probability of eviction of legal owners, which is close to zero. Indeed, when farmers were asked to indicate the major benefits of having secure title, "protection from eviction" was suggested by a majority of the farmers. According to these farmers, the dominant advantage of having secure ownership is improved access to credit.

A critical examination of the study shows that it is fraught with various problems. To start with, a study that seeks to examine the link between ownership security or registration and accessibility to formal credit for investment in land-based activities is comparing two groups of farmers – one group being legal private owners of their land, the ownership of which has been formalised or registered and another group of farmers who do not own the land; that is, they are squatters. This simply amounts to, for example, comparing an *elephant* with a *table* without any common denominator. Thus, how can such a study come out with any credible and convincing results? One would have thought that the comparison should have been between two groups of legal landowners but one group with registered or secure ownership and the other group with unregistered ownership or without secure ownership.

Secondly, it is also obvious that the study is not even about secure ownership and insecure occupancy of land by squatters or insecure land ownership. As will be established later, the risk of losing land is an element of ownership insecurity and in fact, the respondents in the study measure landownership insecurity in terms of possible evictions. However, the authors themselves admit that evictions from state land are rare due to the high political cost that the government is likely to suffer if evictions are carried out. Thus, for political expediency, squatters are rarely evicted from state land. Indeed, from the statistics provided by the authors, the probability that a squatter *will not be evicted during his lifetime is 92.5%*! Thus, even without formalised or registered landownership or certificates of utilisation, there is security.

Thirdly, the study of Feder and Onchan is not about the link between secure landownership or land registration and access to formal credit. The study is rather about the lending behaviour of banking institutions; that is, how such institutions treat two groups of farmers. A bank may accept only registered title as collateral for granting loans based on its internal rules and regulations but this does not mean that unregistered title is insecure or registered title implies security. Security of ownership as a concept will be explained in detail in chapter three where it will become clear that premised on the meaning of security, it cannot or is not determined by banks. Indeed, the authors themselves have acknowledged in their study that squatters on government land (that is, the de facto landowners) are protected as evictions are rare. Thus, there is security of landownership even though banks may not be willing to grant loans based on such ownership as collateral. In conclusion, it is obvious from a critical analysis of Feder and Onchan's (1987) study that albeit they claimed to have established the necessary evidence, the study did not actually establish any evidence.

Despite the above problematic and unsustainable argument regarding secure ownership or registered title serving as collateral for formal credit for investment purposes, the security-collateral argument continues to dominate the literature. Indeed, it reached its crescendo following the publication of de Soto's book in 2000 where he enunciated his so called "dead capital" thesis. Extensive quotations of the relevant portions of the book on the issue are necessary to put the ensuing critical analysis of the thesis in perspective. De Soto (2000, pp.27-30) writes:

> Over the past decade, my researchers, assisted by knowledgeable local professionals, have made surveys of five Third World cities - Cairo, Lima, Manila, Mexico City and Port-au-Prince – in an effort to gauge the value of possessions of those people who have been locked out of the capitalised economy by discriminatory laws......To be more confident of our results, we focused our attention on the most tangible and detectable assets: real estate.
>
> Unlike the sale of food or shoes, auto repair, or the manufacture of phoney Cartier watches- activities that are difficult to count and even more difficult to value – buildings cannot be hidden. You can ascertain their value simply by surveying the cost of the building materials and observing the selling prices of comparable buildings. We spent many thousands of days counting buildings block by block.....In collaboration with people on the spot we tested and retested our methods and results.
>
> We discovered that the way the people build in the undercapitalised sector takes as many forms as there are legal obstacles to circumvent. The most obvious examples are the shanties built on government owned land. But our researchers discovered far more creative ways of getting around the real estate laws. In Peru, for instance, people formed agricultural cooperatives to buy estates from their old owners and to convert them into housing and industrial settlements. Because there are no easy legal ways to change land tenure, farmers in state-own cooperatives illegally subdivided the land into smaller, privately held parcels. As a result, few if

> any have valid title to their ground. In Port-au-Prince even quite expensive properties change hands without anybody bothering to inform the registry office, which is hopelessly backlogged any way. In Manila, housing springs up on land zoned solely for industrial use. In Cairo, residents of older four-storey public housing projects build illegal storeys on top of their buildings and sell the apartments to relatives and other clients………..
>
> ……There still may be deeds or some kind of record in someone's hands, but the real ownership status of these assets has slipped out of the official registry system, leaving records and maps outdated. The result is that most people's resources are commercially and financially invisible. Nobody really knows who owns what and where, who is accountable for the performance of obligations, who is responsible for losses and fraud, and what mechanisms are available to enforce payment for services and goods delivered. Consequently, most potential assets in these countries have not been identified or realised; there is little accessible capital and the exchange economy is constrained and sluggish. This picture of the undercapitalised sector is strikingly different from the conventional wisdom of the developing world. But this is where most people live. It is a world where ownership of assets is difficult to trace and validate and is governed by no legally recognisable set of rules; the assets' potentially useful economic attributes have not been described or organised; where they cannot be used to obtain surplus value through multiple transactions because their unfixed nature and uncertainty leave too much room for misunderstanding, faulty recollection and reversal of agreement. Where most assets, in short, are dead capital.

According to de Soto, based on the valuation they carried out in their study, the "dead capital" of four of the countries in which the case study cities are located are as follows: Haiti (the country in which Port-au Prince is located) - US$5.2 billion; Peru (for Lima) - US$74 billion; Philippines (for Manila) - US$133 billion; and Egypt (for Cairo) - US$240 billion. The author asserts that based on the data from these four countries that they studied a projection was then made to arrive at the "dead capital" of Africa (US$0.97 trillion) and Asia (US$2.33 trillion). Based on these projections, he observes that the "dead capital" of the Third World and former communist nations is US$9.34 trillion.

Contrariwise, de Soto notes that "In the West every asset – every piece of land, every house, every chattel - is formally fixed in updated records governed by rules contained in the property system" (p.46). As a result of this, he explicates that in the developing world and former communist nations, property serves a physical purpose whilst in the West or developed world it serves as capital outside its physical purpose as it can be used as collateral to access formal credit. De Soto, therefore, asserts that capitalism has triumphed in the West and by implication making it rich because of comprehensive land registration but the advanced nations seem unable to teach the rest of the world. On the other hand, he attributes the undercapitalised nature of the economies of the developing world (and by implication the existence of poverty in pandemic proportions) to the fact that a lot of landed property ownership is unregistered. He observes: "Why assets can be made to produce abundant capital in the West but very little in the rest of the world is a mystery" (p.37).

The implication of de Soto's thesis is two-fold. First of all, the poor in the developing world possess "dead capital" (landed property that is unregistered) but which becomes "alive" when registered thereby enabling owners of the property to use it as collateral to obtain formal capital for wealth creation via investment. It therefore means that the ability of landed property owners to access formal credit for wealth creation is solely dependent on registration; once somebody's landed property is registered he/she automatically gains access to credit from financial institutions for investment and wealth creation. The "dead capital" thesis has been heralded globally. Mahama (2008), for example, claims that the "dead capital" locked up in landed property in Ghana is worth US$ 8-10 billion. Indeed, there is now an International Commission on Legal Empowerment of the Poor whose main aim seems to be the spreading of the idea that land registration is a necessary aspect of poverty reduction in the developing world (Bromley, 2008, cited in Abdulai and Hammond, 2010).

However, a critical analysis of the entire research findings of de Soto shows that his pronouncements are personal opinions uncorroborated with evidence. To begin with, just like the study of Feder and Onchan (1987) already examined above, de Soto's work is not about the relationship between landed property ownership registration on one hand and accessibility to formal credit and investment behaviour of owners of registered real estate on the other. It is rather about the behaviour of "illegal" and true real estate owners towards real estate laws. Even here, there is no evidence in the work to the effect that real estate owners cannot use their property as collateral to access formal credit from financial institutions because the ownership is unregistered in his case study areas which are five developing world cities - Cairo, Lima, Manila, Mexico City and Port-au-Prince. What de Soto and his team of researchers did is that they spent thousands of days counting buildings in the case study cities and, supposedly, valuing them but managed to confidently conclude that it is real estate ownership registration that determines access to formal capital in both the developing and developed world. Obviously, such a conclusion is a personal opinion and not based on the research de Soto and his team conducted.

Secondly, there is no shred of empirical evidence in de Soto's work to show that in the developed world every landed property is registered and that capitalism has triumphed in such a continent because of comprehensive landed property ownership registration systems. The case study areas covered four cities in the developing world, yet he arrived at such a conclusion with certitude. Indeed, such an assertion is grossly erroneous. Admittedly in advanced countries like Belgium, Netherlands, Germany, Denmark, Sweden, and Switzerland there is 100% coverage of ownership registration (Cadastral Template, 2003). However, there other countries that do not have 100% coverage. In Japan for instance, the coverage in terms of urban landed property ownership is 72% whilst in Portugal out of 17,000,000 urban land parcels, 2,055,000 are registered constituting 12% coverage (Cadastral Template, 2003).

Furthermore, in England and Wales, 26% of landed property ownership is currently unregistered; this percentage represents the national average and in some counties it ranges from 35% to 53% (HM Land Registry, 2011). However, Britain and Japan are members of the G8 - the world's most capitalised and industrialised nations that account for about 65% of the world's economy. More importantly, England took the lead in industrial revolution that occurred several years ago before it spread to other European countries and the factors that accounted for Britain's lead were availability of technology, government prodding and a large and varied trade network (partly due to colonization) (Harvie, 1993) and not real estate registration. Indeed, under the current land registration legislation in England and Wales (Land Registration Act 2002) a mortgage transaction is one of the events that trigger land registration and it is upon the occurrence of the event that registration becomes mandatory. Thus, for mortgage purposes, land registration is a post-requirement and not a prerequisite.

Thirdly, de Soto identified every landed property that its ownership had not been registered and using the cost and comparative methods of valuation, supposedly valued such properties in order to gauge the value of possessions of those people who have been locked out of the capitalised economy. From the statistics provided in his work, even though they surveyed five cities, they ultimately valued the properties in four cities. Apart from the fact that the actual processes that went into the valuation process have not been explained, the total number of such properties for each city has not been given, neither has the total value for the properties for each city been provided. What have been provided are rather the total values for each country and there are no statistics on the number of unregistered properties for each of the countries. However, based on these values, those of Africa, Asia and the developing world as whole, plus former communist nations have been reckoned. Here again, there is no evidence on the total number of unregistered landed properties in Africa, Asia, the whole of the developing world and former communist nations. The bases or parameters used in the computations have not also been explained.

But even granted that the computations of the so called "dead capital" are correct and reliable, the assertions of de Soto are full of contradictions. He claims that when landed property is unregistered, it is commercially and financially invisible and that its value cannot be realised. However, his own research findings shows that in Port-au-Prince expensive landed properties change hands without anybody bothering to inform the registry office and in Cairo, residents of older four-storey public housing projects build illegal storeys on top of their buildings and sell the apartments to relatives and other clients. Thus, certainly, unregistered real estate (even illegally property) is bought and sold and when it is traded its value is realised.

Furthermore, from the statistics regarding the percentage of unregistered landed property ownership in England and Wales provided above for example, does it mean that such landed properties are commercially and financially invisible and their values cannot be realised or they cannot be used as collateral for loans? It is common knowledge that they are not. As already noted, in England and Wales, under the Land Registration Act 2002, land registration is a post-requirement and not a prerequisite for mortgage purposes. Also, under the same law, sale of real estate is one of the events that trigger land registration and it is after the sale that the purchaser is legally required to register the property within two months from the date of sale. Thus, where the property has never been registered, it will be registered for the first time in the name of the purchaser after the sale. Landed property therefore does not need to be registered before it can be traded and for its value to be realised.

Finally, de Soto also claims from his research that when real estate is not registered nobody really knows who owns what and where and who is responsible for the performance of obligations. It is an undeniable fact that before the buying and selling or the trading of any asset takes place, the potential purchaser would have to in the first instance, identify the owner or his agent as the case may be. So granted that when real estate is unregistered, nobody actually knows who owns what and where and who is responsible for the performance of obligations, how can expensive properties in Port-au-Prince be traded between sellers and buyers as established by de Soto in his research? Similarly how can residents in Cairo trade "illegal" apartments? Thus, the evidence he himself has provided sharply contradicts his conclusions.

It is therefore not surprising that authors like Gilbert (2002) and Fernandes (2002) have criticised de Soto's methodology and supporting research and therefore disputed his argument. In spite of the loopholes and contradictions in de Soto's work, which have been laid bare in the preceding discourse, for the wrong reasons, his so called "dead capital" thesis has been heralded globally. It appears that people hastily read de Soto's work without any reflection or perhaps because it fits nicely into the predilections of his apologists. But what is the evidence from empirical research on the link between land registration on one hand and accessibility to formal credit and investment behaviour of owners of registered landed property on the other?

Evidence abounds in the developing world and elsewhere, which shows that there is no discernible link between land registration and access to formal credit for investment. No study in Peru has been able to establish a direct causation between land registration and increased extension of credit, since the main cause for loan rejection by financial institutions is low repayment capacity of the borrower rather than lack of collateral in the form of registered landed property (Angel et al. 2006). Research in Mexico has shown that there has been no increase in access to formal credit by newly registered landed property owners (Angel et al. 2006), which is reinforced by a study that established that Mexican owners of registered land have little interest in formal credit, preferring loans from friends or relatives (Durand-Lasserve and Payne, 2006). A study conducted in Lima established same evidence (Gravois, 2005). It is interesting to note that the study of de Soto covered these same cities. Based on the flawed and contradictory nature of de Soto's study as shown supra, is it not astounding that the research findings of Durand-Lasserve and Payne, Gravois and Angel et al. on the same issue are completely the opposite of de Soto's findings in the same case study areas.

Reinforcing the above research findings, in Buenos Aires, access to formal credit from banks has not increased significantly after land registration whilst in Paraguay land registration has not improved access to formal credit by the least wealthy households (Durand-Lasserve and Payne, 2006; Carter and Olinto, 2003). In Lac Alaotra – Madagascar, land registration has not been able to open up formal credit opportunities for farmers due to their low income levels (Jacoby and Minten, 2005). A study in Argentina that compared the effect of land registration on access to loans from financial institutions in identical settlements – one with registered landed property and the other with unregistered landed property appeared equally modest (Galiani and Shargrodsky, 2005 and 2004). Regarding Kenya, Migot-Adholla (1994), Green (1987), Bruce (1986), and Okoth- Ogendo (1982) established that there was no relationship between land registration and investment in land related activities. The findings of Bruce and Migot-Adholla (1994) in Ghana, Senegal, Uganda, Burkina-Faso and Somalia and Firmin-Sellers and Sellers (1999) in Cameroon also indicate no link between land title registration and investment in land. Other studies have shown that land registration has little or no impact on either investment or farm income (Firmin-Sellers and Sellers, 1999; Migot Adholla et al., 1994; Pinckney and Kimuyu, 1994; Migot-Adholla, 1993; Atwood, 1990; Carter and Wiebe, 1990; Bruce, 1986; Green, 1987; Okoth-Ogendo, 1982), something that is often mirrored by similar findings for urban areas (Durand-Lasserve and Royston, 2000) and especially, investment in housing improvements (Payne, 1997; Varley, 1987).

Examining the impact of land registration on access to formal credit in Ghana, Abdulai and Hammond (2010) have identified the determinants of formal credit accessibility to be: (a) financial capability, which can partly be measured in terms of the level of interest rates charged by banks and credit records or financial information; (b) availability of business plans to support loan requests; (c) availability of collateral in the form of landed property; (d) location and quality or standard of landed property to be used as collateral; (e) willingness of insurance companies to insure the landed property to be used as collateral; and (f) documentation of ownership in the form of title deeds (not necessarily registered title deeds) as opposed to "petits papiers" (small papers) like land allocation notes/papers or land transfer receipts. Abdulai and Hammond established that financial capability is the overarching determinant. The study of Barrows and Roth (1990) on the constraints to formal credit is illuminating. In terms of farmers who want to access formal credit to invest in commercial farming, they established that banks generally do not wish to become farmers and so unless there is a viable land market, they are unwilling to accept land in general as collateral even when the landownership is registered.

Various studies conducted by the International Institute for Environment and Development (IIED) across Africa shows that employment and income level are the key factors that determine the ability of people to obtain loans from financial institutions and the poor are reluctant to use their registered landed property as collateral because of the risk of foreclosure of their property is too high (IIED, 2006). The poor in the developing world are reluctant to borrow from banks, as the banks are reluctant to lend to the poor due to the fact that: (a) household incomes are often too low for financial institutions to be interested in lending; (b) cost of managing small credit is too high as compared with returns; and (c) low market value of the property to be mortgaged due to inappropriate location but location determines value (Durand-Lasserve and Payne, 2006; Payne, 2001).

The overwhelming evidence from the above discourse shows that there is no discernible link between land registration on one hand and access to capital for investment, wealth creation and development on the other. Various factors determine the ability of an individual to access formal capital for investment, of which financial capability is the most important factor. The issue is not about land registration but rather about the behaviour of banking institutions towards people in terms of granting loans to them. Thus, where landed property is even registered, the banks may not accept it as collateral. However, this does not mean that ownership of the landed property is insecure simply because a bank will not accept it as collateral for mortgage purposes. In some countries in the developing world, the emergence of innovative community-based finance institutions that provide business or investment loans premised more on creditworthiness (financial capability), achieved via regular small savings (for example, Grameen Bank in Bangladesh or Banco Sol and FIE in Bolovia) makes the need for landed property as collateral irrelevant (Payne, 2001), let alone registration.

Encapsulating the preceding empirical evidence, Buckley and Kalarickal (2006), aptly conclude that it is a very dangerous thing to promote land registration policies and programmes as the sole solution necessary to solve the problems of the poor and that land registration by itself cannot "unlock" formal capital – land registration will not necessarily result in increased assets of the poor. In the light of this, what are then the actual drivers of investment?

1.4. Real Drivers of Investment

In terms of agricultural investment especially, the impediments in Africa's agricultural sector already referred to supra, are the factors likely to be responsible for the low level of agricultural investment. Thus it is not about insecurity of landownership or non registration of landed property ownership. Any policies or actions that would effectively address these problems or impediments would most certainly become the driving forces of agricultural investment activities. These have already been alluded to in earlier discussions to include ability to invest and government support.

1.4.1. Ability to Invest

The importance of farmers' financial ability to undertake investment activities cannot be ignored. For any investment activity to become a reality, the individuals involved must of necessity possess the means to invest. Ability in this context refers to the possession of sufficient funds required to carry out a given investment activity. Generating sufficient internal funds by farmers could be a very huge challenge especially in Africa due to the fact that: (a) agriculture is still practiced largely on a subsistence basis; (b) farmers are barely able to produce enough to feed themselves; and (c) income levels are low and poverty exists in pandemic proportions. These do not permit individual savings on which people can rely for land-related investment activities. If farmers do not have the funds to invest, it does not matter how conducive the investment climate may be, how secure their landownership is and whether their land has been registered or not. When people are financially capable of investing, they are more likely prepared to take some risks for any investment activities they undertake.

1.4.2. Government Support

The agricultural sector remains the backbone of African economies as it contributes about 60-70% to foreign exchange and employment and 30% to GDP (Breman et al., 2001). It therefore deserves more government attention. One form of government support relates to credit flow to the sector. The extent to which credit flows to farmers is a crucial determinant of how much investment can be undertaken in SSA due to the reason explained above. Availability of alternative sources of funding from financial institutions will enhance ability and willingness to invest. The availability of commercial bank loans may not entirely solve the problems of these farmers. Banks typically grant short term loans, but farmers may require long term facilities to undertake some investments, which have a greater capability of transforming agriculture in SSA. Providing farmers with short term loans to finance long term projects will put them under unnecessary repayment pressure since they may not have alternative income sources from which to repay the loan before their investments begin to yield positive cash flows.

This will require the establishment of specialised financial institutions by governments in countries where they do not exist to provide longer term credit with conditions that are flexible to serve the peculiar needs of farmers. Admittedly such institutions exist in some countries in the sub-continent but the problem appears to be that: (a) over the years the institutions have failed to concentrate on their core business of channelling funds to the agricultural sector and rather operate like private commercial banks; and (b) politicians sometimes interfere in the operations of the institutions. Thus, where such institutions already exist, there is the need for them to concentrate on their core business and there should be minimal political interferences. The agricultural sector has distinct features from the services and manufacturing sectors and therefore agricultural credit should not be fashioned in the same way as the others. Leaving the financing of agriculture in the hands of non specialist commercial banks will not bring about any significant breakthrough in Africa. Of course governments in Africa could also consider providing direct funding for the sector as this is required if the sector is to become successful in leading the fight against poverty. The direct funding could take the form of providing agricultural implements at subsidised prices.

In terms of financing the agricultural sector, international donor community support is also required to supplement whatever is done by national governments. This could take the form of implementing appropriate programmes that would specifically benefit small scale farmers. An example of the type of international intervention advocated here is the programme to be implemented by the US government that is aimed at enhancing food security in Northern Ghana. Under the programme, which is to be implemented through the United States Agency for International Development (USAID), over 860,000 vulnerable women, children and family members, mostly small scale farmers, would be assisted over the next five years to improve upon their agriculture production to help fight hunger and to alleviate poverty (GNA, 2011). The programme is part of "Feed the Future" Project, which is a US$3.5 billion US government's global hunger and food security initiative to support country-driven approaches to address the root causes of poverty, hunger, and under nutrition (GNA, 2011).

The support of governments is also required in the area of socio-economic infrastructure. In this regard, governments' investment is required in the area of irrigation facilities because agriculture has remained rain-fed in most parts of Africa. The percentage of land under irrigation in Africa is lower than what exists in Asia and Asia also has a more reliable source of water supply than Africa (Dorward, 2002). Provision of irrigation facilities will reduce the overdependence on rainfall for production, thus reducing the risk of losses arising from bad weather conditions.

The other area that requires the support of governments is transportation. A high amount of post harvest losses is experienced by most African farmers as a result of the poor road network linking the rural areas to the urban and peri-urban market centres. The density of paved roads in Africa in the 1990's is said to be far lower compared to that of India during its green revolution in the 1960's and transport cost as a consequence is higher in Africa than Asia (Dorward et al., 2002) and this does not appear to have changed significantly up to date. Investment that will significantly improve rural road network will reduce related losses and make agricultural investments more profitable.

There is also the need for governments to invest in storage facilities and agro-processing. This will reduce the impact of the presence of the cobweb phenomenon explained earlier. Agro-processing will provide ready markets for farm produce and reduce price fluctuations. Storage facilities will also allow farmers to regulate supply more effectively and this will reduce price fluctuations. The combined effect of this will be a key factor in reducing agricultural risk and enhancing farmers' access to formal credit and willingness to invest. Government support is thus required to address the very basic and core problems experienced by farmers in Africa. These constraints make agriculture so risky, lower investment returns, and make farming unprofitable and unattractive to both farmers and formal lending institutions.

Most countries that experienced the green revolution were associated with a number of internal policy decisions, which increased agricultural investment and productivity. According to Dorward et al. (2002) almost every agricultural transformation in the past has been linked to local research and extension services, irrigation, investment in infrastructure, intervention in price stabilisation and subsidised input and credit supply of some sort. Figure 1.3 below illustrates the systematic steps that governments could adopt to transform agriculture in Africa and it is important to note that the impact of these interventions could be huge irrespective of whether there is security or insecurity or whether landed property is registered or not.

As Dorward et al. (2002) explains the process of agricultural transformation shown in Figure 1.3 begins with the provision of a sound infrastructural base. In the second phase of intervention, governments need to ensure that reliable input and output markets exist. They also need to provide some amount of financial assistance to farmers. This would ensure that farmers have a more reliable source of income. After nurturing the sector up to stage two, governments would have succeeded in transforming the agricultural sector into a profitable venture that would become more attractive to the private sector commercial banks. This would then pave the way for governments to withdraw any direct support from the sector.

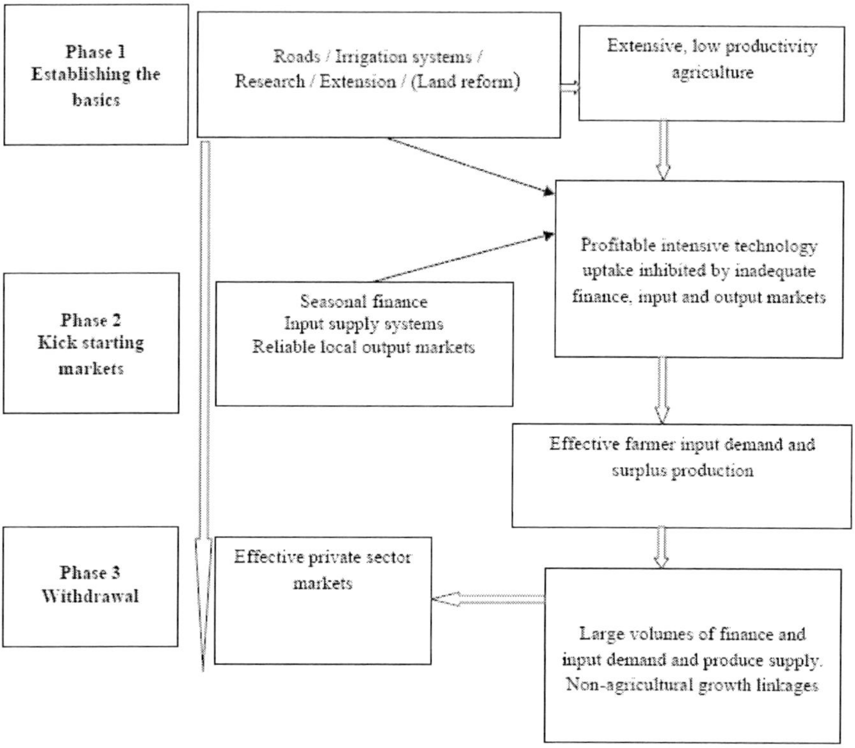

Source: Dorward et al. (2002).

Figure 1.3. The Process of Agricultural Transformation.

1.5. Definition of Sub-Saharan Africa

Sub-Saharan Africa (SSA), by the World Bank definition refers to countries south of the Sahara. They are therefore countries that are not part of North Africa (Western Sahara, Morocco, Algeria, Tunisia, Libya and Egypt) but include offshore islands. Thus, SSA comprises 48 countries, which are: *Lusophone countries* (5) where the official language is Portuguese – Angola,

Guinea Bissau, Sao Tome and Principe, Cape Verde and Mozambique; *Francophone countries* (11) - Benin, Togo, Ivory Coast, Burkina Faso, Senegal, Niger, Mali, Gabon, Guinea, Congo and Democratic Republic of Congo where French is the official language; *Anglophone countries* (14) where English is the official language - Ghana, Nigeria, South Africa, Sierra Leone, Liberia, Gambia, Zimbabwe, Zambia, Namibia, Botswana, Lesotho, Kenya, Uganda and Mauritius; and *Anglo-Francophone countries* (2) where the official languages are English and French – Cameroon and Seychelles. The *residual group* comprises 16 countries. They are the following with their official languages: Chad- Arabic and French; Mauritania - Arabic; Eritrea – English, Arabic and Tingriya; Djibouti and Comoros – French and Arabic; Madagascar – French and Malagasy; Somalia – Somali and Arabic; Swaziland – Swati and English; Tanzania – English and Swahili; Sudan - Arabic; Ethiopia – Amharic and English; Equatorial Guinea – Spanish and French, Central African Republic – French and Sango; Burindi – French and Kirundi; Rwanda – French, English and Kinyarwanda; and Malawi – English and Chichewa. The geographical location of SSA is shown in Figure 1.4 below.

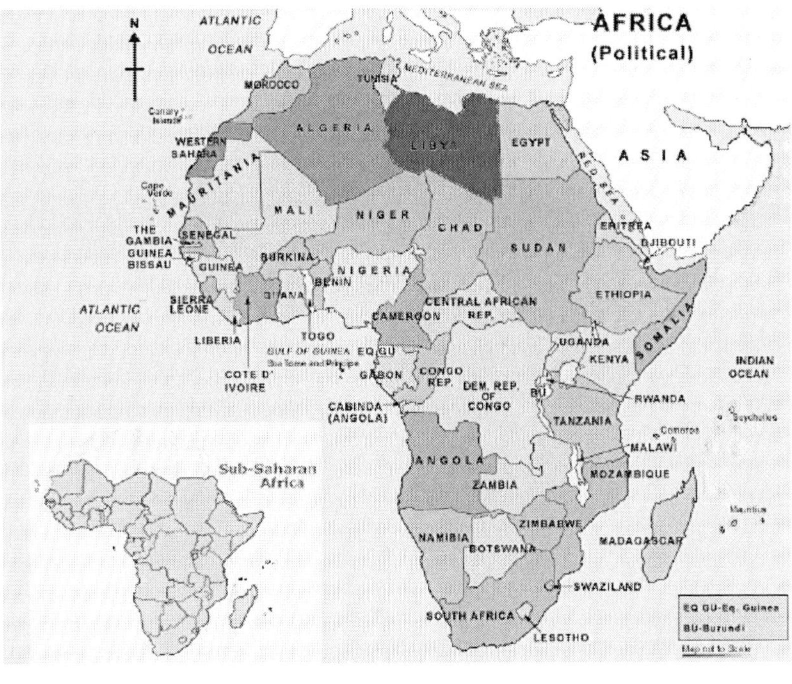

Figure 1.4. Map of SSA.

Conclusion

This chapter has examined the link between land registration and landed property ownership security. It has also examined the nexus between ownership security and land registration on one hand and investment, wealth creation and development on the other. The overwhelming empirical evidence adduced from various studies shows that ownership security cannot be assured via land registration and indeed, in some cases it can be a source of insecurity. Regarding the link between ownership security and investment, the importance of ownership security has been over hiked. Ownership security alone cannot guarantee investment; there are other important determinants of investment activities, the most critical determinant being ability to invest which is also determined by financial capability. Furthermore, the established evidence suggests that there is no discernible link between land registration and access to formal credit for investment, wealth creation and development.

Having set the appropriate scene, the rest of the book is structured in the following manner. Chapter two explains the theory of property rights. In this chapter, the areas considered include: explanation, systems, and economic importance of property rights; and origins of, and development of landed property rights among ethnic groups in SSA. In chapter three, the bases of the argument that equates land registration to ownership security are subjected to critical analyses. In doing this, the chapter defines ownership security, explains the forms of land registration systems that exist globally, identifies and explains the right and critical role that land registration is supposed to play in the economies of countries, and defines the actual determinants of real estate ownership security. Summary and policy implications and contained in the last chapter.

Chapter 2

PROPERTY RIGHTS THEORY

ABSTRACT

This chapter discusses the theory of property rights in order to provide an appropriate theoretical or conceptual framework for this book. The discussion shows that ownership of any form of property or asset is not about physical ownership; rather it refers to the exercise of rights over the property and full ownership corresponds to the exercise of a bundle of 12 different strands of rights. In terms of landed property, when a person can exercise more than one right over the property, it is referred to as an *interest*, which is normally represented by *title*. There are two forms of property rights, which are private and public property rights. The importance of property rights in economics cannot be over-emphasized as they play a crucial role in internalising externalities and allocating scarce resources.

Regarding the origin of property rights, two philosophical theories are often used to explain it and these theories are the first occupancy and labour theories. The theories have been applied to explicate the origin and development of landed property rights among ethnic groups in SSA. Such property rights are referred to as traditional systems of property rights or landed property ownership and they are often: (a) perceived as communal, which do not permit individual ownership; and (b) considered as deities that cannot be traded. These perceptions have also been examined in this chapter and the conclusion is that there is a gross misunderstanding about the way the systems operate in practice and therefore the perceptions are misplaced.

2.1. Introduction

Undeniably, the institutional arrangements under which a person gains access to landed property to a large extent, determines among other things, his or her ability to undertake improvements on the property. Landed property ownership systems therefore exercise dominant control over the property, the manner in which labour and capital are applied to it and the distribution of the rewards emanating from its use (West, 2000, p.1). It is thus important to understand the way existing landed property ownership systems operate. As earlier noted, countries of SSA have been subject to colonialism - indigenous landed property ownership systems therefore operate alongside alien systems (formal systems) imposed by colonial governments. Consequently, a dual system of landed property ownership system exists in most countries in SSA.

Landed property ownership is about property rights. Thus it is expedient to first of all discuss the theory of property rights and its application to landed property since it offers a better understanding of ownership. This will then lead to an examination of the development of the landed property ownership systems that obtained prior to the advent of colonial rule - that is, the long periods of settlement by indigenous ethnic groups and the social patterns, which emerged over many centuries. Section two is devoted to an explanation of property rights whilst section three looks at the systems of property rights. The origin and economic importance of property rights are discussed in sections four and five respectively. The theories on the origin of property rights considered in section four are applied to the development of landed property rights amongst ethnic groups in SSA in section six whilst section seven deals with conclusion.

2.2. An Explanation of Property Rights

One popular conception views property as *things*. Therefore property is seen as tangible things like land, houses, automobiles, tools, factories as well as intangible things like patents and trademarks (Munzer, 1990). Another way of comprehending property is the legal conception of property, which is very common among lawyers. The legal conception understands property as *relations*. Property, therefore, consists of legal relations among persons or entities with respect to things (Munzer, 1990). From both conceptions of property, it is clear that property consists of corporeal and incorporeal hereditaments; thus, legal arrangements or contracts are a form of property. As rightly put by Alchian (1965), if one concentrates his or her attention on constraints and classes of permissible action he or she finds himself or herself studying the *property* aspect of behaviour.

According to Becker (1977, p.8) even though the term "right" has multiple meanings and is so deeply entrenched in both ordinary and technical usages, when moral philosophers contrast rights with ideals, personal or social goods and virtues, what they mean by the term "right" seems to be something like this: "The existence of a right is the existence of a state of affairs in which one person (the right-holder) has a claim on an act or forbearance from another person (the duty-bearer) in the sense that, should the claim be exercised or in force and the act or forbearance not be done, it would be justifiable, other things being equal, to use coercive measures to extract either the performance required or compensation in lieu of that performance…"

The above definition of a right encompasses various elements including the notion of duty, coercion and the fact that it may be concerned with acts or omissions and also the fact that violations require restitution. Combining the explanation of a right and property, Hallowell (1943) has defined property rights as: "a system of relations between individuals … it involves rights, duties, powers, privileges and forbearance of certain kinds" whilst Bromley (1991) has explained a property right as a claim to a benefit or income stream that the state will agree to protect via the assignment of duty to others who may covet or somehow interfere with the benefit stream. According to de Alessi and Staaf (1989, p.179) property rights are the rights of individuals to the use of resources. Thus property rights are simply rights of ownership and refer to the legal and social relations among people in a society with respect to ownership of property.

Consequently, ownership of property defines claim rights, privileges and powers the owner of the property has as well as the duties such ownership imposes on him as the owner and other members of the society in relation to the property. In the light of this, an owner of property expects community members to prevent other people from interfering with his or her actions providing that these actions are not prohibited in the specifications of his or her property rights (Demsetz, 1967, p. 347). Thus if Emma has the right to possess a thing, not only that other people do not have the right to the thing, but they have a duty not to interfere with the possession of Emma – perhaps even to see to it that the thing is restored to Emma when lost (Becker, 1977, p.21). The claim rights, privileges, powers and duties defined by property ownership are further explicated using Hohfeld's Fundamental Legal

Conceptions, normally referred to as Hohfeldian analysis of property. The Table below shows the Fundamental Legal Conceptions.

Table 2.1. Hohfeld's Fundamental Legal Conceptions

Elements	Correlatives	Opposites
Claim right	Duty	No-Right
Privilege (Liberty)	No-Right	Duty
Power	Liability	Disability (No-Power)
Immunity	Disability	Liability

Source: Munzer, 1990, p.19.

As Munzer (1990) has explained, if for example Kombian is the owner of a given property, he is entitled to exercise his claim rights, but it is his duty to ensure that in the exercise of his right, he does not interfere with the rights of others. Ownership of property also confers a privilege, which is a legal liberty or freedom. The freedom to deal with the property involves not a correlative duty but the absence of a right (no-right) on someone else's part to interfere in the exercise of the privilege. A person has a legal power when by some act he can alter his position as an owner or that of somebody else. The correlative for power is liability, the susceptibility to having one's legal position altered. Kombian as the owner has the power to deal with his property the way he desires. If he decides to transfer it to Konlan by signing certain documents, Kombian has the power of transfer and Konlan a correlative liability to receive. Finally, immunity is the lack of susceptibility to having one's legal position altered by someone else. Its correlative is the absence of power in someone else to alter one's legal position in the way protected by the immunity. If Konlan cannot legally compel Kombian to sell his property to him, Kombian has immunity with respect to Konlan's forcing a sale of the property. Correlatively, Konlan has no power to force the sale.

It is based on this Hohfeldian analysis of property that models (also referred to as power tools) relating to property have been developed – the Rights, Obligations and Responsibilities (ROR) model; the Rights, Responsibilities, Revenues (benefits) and Relationships (Four Rs) model; and the Rights, Responsibilities, Restrictions, Revenues and Relationships (Five Rs) model. The Four Rs model or tool, for instance is used to demonstrate or show stakeholder roles when they collaborate in the management of natural resources in a sustainable fashion. The model emphasises the need for an assessment of the Four Rs since it is their balance that indicates the underlying power structures and current incentives or disincentives to achieving sustainable use of natural resources (IIED, 2005). The tool is useful in various situations including: (a) the analysis of multi-stakeholder situations and the diagnosis of problems; (b) the assessment and comparison of policies; (c) in role negotiation process, institutional re-structuring, and decentralisation; and (d) as an evaluation tool in the project cycle and a training methodology (IIED, 2005).

Honoré (1961) observes that full ownership of property refers to the ownership of a bundle of 12 different rights: (a) right to possess (exclusive control); (b) right to use (usufruct); (c) right to manage; (d) right to income; (e) right to capital; (f) right to security; (g) right to transmissibility; (h) right to divisibility; (i) prohibition of harmful use; (j) absence of term (duration); (k) liability to execution; and (l) residual character (reversionary right).

However, Honoré is quick to add that albeit all the above strands of rights constitute full ownership, none of them is a necessary constituent of ownership per se since people may be said to own property in various restricted senses. For example, Daniel might have the right to manage and receive income from his house but due to a leasing agreement, he has restricted rights to use and exclusive possession. Consequently, the bundle of rights can be split into lesser bundles, all of which can be owned. Different people might have different rights existing in a particular property at the same time and so the rights of one person may be subject to constraints set by the rights of other members of the society. It is in the light of this that Lund (2008, p.15) notes that the idea of ownership as "total exclusion of the right of any other individual in the universe" is precisely an *idea* since in concrete societies, African and "Western" ownership is always circumscribed by other people's rights limiting the exercise of the abstract total right to property.

Property rights as a concept is applicable to all forms of assets - real and personal. Personal property refers to tangible assets like washing machines and cars (corporeal hereditaments) as well as intangible property (incorporeal hereditaments) like patents, which explains why intellectual property rights exist. Real property is also a tangible asset and connotes land and/or the developments on it. Its other name, as earlier noted is landed property or real estate. The focus of this book is on landed property or real estate and its registration. Based on the theory of property rights, ownership of landed property is not about the physical ownership but rather the rights exercisable by the owner over the property. When a person can exercise two or more rights over landed property, they are referred to as an *interest* in the property, which is normally described as *title* to the landed property. Thus landed property *title* simply refers to ownership of the property.

Hobbes (1951) has imagined a state of nature in which there is no acknowledgement of what is "mine" and "thine" no acceptance of boundaries among persons, no law and no conventions; in this Hobbesian state, the life of a person is "nasty, brutish and short". As Becker (1977), Buchannan (1975) and Hardin (1968) note, it is obviously due to the fact that in using the property that is not owned by anybody, it would be "free for all" and therefore there would be hostilities and would also lead to overexploitation and misuse of the property. Thus, to prevent this situation, there is the need for property rights to define the claim rights, privileges, powers and duties of persons regarding the use of property and resources in general.

Property rights are normally enforced by formal mechanisms like the legal system and social customs and or attitudes concerning the legitimacy and recognition of property rights (Taylor, 1988). Thus, the level of noise, the choices individuals make regarding the kind of clothes to wear and how to talk, our intrusion on other people's privacy are restricted or restrained not merely by laws backed by the police force, but by social acceptance, reciprocity and voluntary social ostracism for violators of accepted codes of conduct (De Alessi and Staaf, 1989; Alchian, 1965). These formal and informal rules combined define a system of property rights. In the words of Alessi (1980, p.3), "The system of property rights adopted within a community provides a mechanism for assigning to particular individuals the authority to select how specific resources will be used, given classes of non-prohibited uses.....In particular it specifies the nature of the rights, which an individual may hold to the use of resources, to the income generated for those resources and to the transferability of those resources to other individuals".

2.3. Systems of Property Rights

2.3.1. Public Property Rights System

Public property rights refer to the rights that are exercised by all members of the community or public. Communal ownership means that the community denies the individual citizens, the right to interfere with any person's exercise of communally owned rights (Demsetz, 1967). Public ownership is borne by all members of the public and no member can divest himself of that ownership. A member of the community therefore holds the right by virtue of the fact that he belongs to that community and so if he decides to relinquish his membership, he or she loses the right. When land, for example, is communally owned, every individual has the right to hunt, till or mine the land. Normally, communal ownership fails to concentrate the cost associated with any person's exercise of his communal right on that person (Demsetz, 1967) and this is because in communal ownership, the costs of any decision or choice are less fully thrust upon the selector than under private property (Alchian, 1967, p.827).

Taking land for example, a person seeking to maximize the exercise of his communal land rights will tend to over hunt or over till the land since some of the costs of his or her actions are borne by other members of the community. Thus, the stock of game and the fertility of the soil will diminish so fast. Of course, every member of the community who owns these rights can negotiate and agree to reduce the rate at which they work on the land, but this negotiation comes with costs. Negotiation or transaction costs will be high here since it will be difficult for many persons to reach a mutually satisfactory agreement, especially when each member of the community has the right to work on the land as fast as he or she so pleases.

Demsetz (1967, p.215) expresses this disadvantage of communal property rights system in the following words: "Communal property results in great externalities. The full costs of the activities of an owner of a communal property right are not borne directly by him, nor can they be called to his attention easily by the willingness of others to pay him an appropriate sum. Communal property rules out 'pay-to-use-the-property' system and high negotiation and policing costs make ineffective a 'pay-him-not-to-use-the-property' system". According to Milgrom and Roberts (1992, p.295) and Libecap (1989, p.22-23), the costs are even likely to be higher when the group is larger or when members of the community are not homogenous. As early as the ancient times, Aristotle (384-322 BC) noticed the disadvantage in communal ownership of property rights when he observed: "That which is common to the greatest number has the least care bestowed upon it. Everyone thinks chiefly of his own, hardly at all of the common interest".

2.3.2. Private Property Rights System

A private property right is an assignment of exclusive authority to an individual to the use of property deemed to be his or her private property (Alchian, 1967). In other words, the private owner has an unrestricted right to the use of the property. In private property rights regime, other members of the community recognize the right of the private owner to exclude them from exercising his or her private individual rights. Alchian (1967, p.818) observes:

> To say I have private property rights is to say that no one else has the right to make the choice of use of that good (contained in the class of private property). This means that if I select a use for the goods said to be my private property, the selection must not affect the physical attributes of your goods. ...... Private property as I understand it does not imply that a person may use his property in any way he sees fit even if that use will hurt others. Instead, it seems to mean the right to use goods (or to transfer that right) in any way the owner wishes so long as the physical attributes or uses of all other people's private property is unaffected.

The observation of Alchian implies that if some of the uses by private property rights owners negatively affect other people's private property rights, it means that the private property rights are being violated since the use of property by one private owner has denied other people the use of their private properties. Thus although private property rights owners have unrestricted rights to the use of their goods and can use such goods in any manner they want, the rights of other people must equally be respected.

Private property rights owned by different individuals could, for example, be exercised on the same parcel of land. That is, several people may each possess some rights to the use of land at the same time; Daniel could possess the right to grow crops on a given parcel of land whilst Emma has an easement to walk across the same piece of land and each of these private rights may be transferable. Personality theory, which states that the right to private property is integral to the moral development of the person, is often employed to explain the concept of private property rights (Duxbury, 1996). Duxbury uses *Hegel's Philosophy of Right* to describe this theory. The basis of Hegel's argument is that private property is essential for the development of freedom and that it serves as a medium through which the individual becomes a person. Private property is, therefore, the embodiment of personality. Through property, a person's existence is recognised since the respect others show to his property by not trespassing on his or her property reflects their acceptance of him or her as a person.

Utilitarian theory is commonly used to justify private property rights. According to the theory, the average or total happiness of the society cannot be maximised unless there exists rights to appropriate, use and transfer objects of value or interest - in other words, the creation of private property rights is dictated by utility (Ogden, 1931). It emphasises that general welfare would be better served if material resources are owned and controlled by private individuals and firms rather than by the state or the community as a whole; individuals are likely to place a higher value on that which is exclusively their own as compared with that which is owned communally (Duxbury, 1996).

First of all, under private property rights system, the individual owner of the property takes the decision regarding the use of the property and, therefore, incurs the cost of his or her decision. He or she also enjoys the benefit that emanates from the decision he or she takes. Thus, the private property owner does a proper cost-benefit analysis in order to ensure that he or she maximises the benefits or profits of the use to which he or she puts his or her property. Such a decision results in high productivity. Even though, owners normally want to maximise profits in private property rights regime, they are also always very cautious of the decisions they make in production. This is because just as the decisions are profit motivated and they have the right to decide on what to produce and at what price to sell, other members of the society are the users of the end products and equally have the right to decide whether to buy the goods and at what price. By and large, the society determines the profit to be made by the individual property or resource owner. As de Alessi (1980, p.4) puts it, the stronger private property rights are, the closer is the relationship between the welfare of the individual owner and the economic and social consequences of his or her decisions; consequently, the greater is his or her incentive to take account of the benefits and harms of the decision he or she makes.

Secondly, private property rights system internalises externalities at less transaction costs. The development of private rights permits the owner of that private property right to economize regarding the use of those resources from which he or she has the right to exclude others and by doing so much internalization is achieved (Demsetz, 1967, p.216). The owner of private property rights in land, for instance, does not own the rights to land held by other private individuals. Since he or she cannot prevent others from exercising their private rights on the land, he or she has no direct incentive in the absence of negotiations to economize in the use of his or her land in a way that takes into account the effects that his or her actions will have on the land rights of other people. For example, if Daniel constructs a dam on his private land, he does not have any direct incentive to take into account the effects (lower water levels) his action will have on his neighbour's land.

Thus, the same kind of externality that is encountered with communal property rights system is also encountered here, but admittedly, this is to a lesser degree. The externalities that accompany private ownership of property do not affect all owners and generally speaking, it will be necessary for only a few to reach an agreement that takes these effects into account (Demsetz, 1967). If Daniel, an owner of private land, in the process of tilling a parcel of land to grow rice observes Kombian, another owner of private land constructing a dam across a stream on another parcel of land contiguous to his, he (Daniel) might prefer the stream as it is and will ask Kombian to stop the construction of the dam. Kombian might agree to stop the construction of the dam on condition that Daniel pays him. If Daniel accepts and pays Kombian, he will stop. Another alternative is for Daniel to buy off Kombian completely. In either case, it will be a simple negotiation between two parties and the transaction costs here will be low.

However, if Daniel and Kombian were owners of communal land, Kombian might stop the construction of the dam if Daniel pays him but since it is a communal property, Kombian cannot guarantee that another engineer Konlan will not take up the task; Daniel and Kombian have no right to exclude Konlan. This will involve a complex negotiation between Daniel and invariably everyone else and the transaction costs will be very high. Thus, albeit in private property rights system there are also transaction costs, the costs of negotiating an internalization of externalities are reduced considerably. Private property rights system enables users of resources to internalize externalities at less transaction costs and this is because the regime establishes a one-to-one relationship between individual actions and all their effects.

Thirdly, in transactions, it is easier and cheaper to exchange private property than rights that are communal. In communally owned property, it is not legally possible for one person to sell his rights to communal property to other people. Due to the fact that the rights are communally owned, they are not marketable individually. The consent of all the members of the community who own the property must be sought and this is normally a herculean if not an impossible task to perform. Furthermore, it is cheaper and less costly to prepare contracts between individuals as well as the enforcement of such contracts than contracts that involve a lot of people.

Given the advantages of private property rights, it is not surprising that it is an integral part of the legal structure of the European society; it is held to have arisen in opposition to the rules of feudal society, where the local lord had superior rights of ownership and all tenants in the area paid him "feuds" or fees (Payne, 1997). Payne notes that the concept of private ownership of property rights is embodied in English common law as expressed in its purist form in the French Civil Code of 1804-8 that was drafted after the Revolution of 1789 and it is commonly known as the Napoleonic Code since it was imposed on countries, which Napoleon's and later French governments colonized or influenced. Also, the private individual property rights system has been the cornerstone of Western European and American societies for the last two hundred years to the extent that they are commonly known as property owning democracies.

In the developing world, however, private individual ownership and registration of landed property rights in, particular, is largely an imported concept and are most common in urban centres, where they were introduced or strengthened by colonial administration for the benefit of European settlers (Mabogunje, 1990, p.18). This assertion implies that before colonization or in the rural areas in the developing world, the concept of private ownership of property rights in land did not exist or does not exist. However, such an argument is unsustainable - the issue is discussed further later.

2.4. Theories on the Origin of Property Rights

There are two philosophical theories that can be used to explain how property rights originated. They are the first occupancy and labour theories, which are often collectively, referred to as the natural rights theory.

2.4.1. First Occupancy Theory

The first occupancy theory awards ownership of an un-appropriated object to a person who occupies such object first with the intention of appropriating it to himself or herself (Asante, 1975). It is premised on the fact that being there first somehow justifies ownership rights. The Romans called this theory a mode of natural acquisition and Pound (1954, p.109) observes: "taking possession of what one discovers is so in accord with a fundamental human instinct that discovery and occupation have stood in the books ever since substantially as Romans stated them". The theory was a recognized mode of establishing title in Roman law and has persisted throughout legal history as a foundation of property. Kant (1887, p.82) terms this theory the Principle of External Acquisition, which he elaborates as follows: "What I bring under my power according to the Law of external Freedom, of which as an object of my free activity of Will I have the capability of making use according to the Postulate of the Practical Reason, and which I will to become mine in conformity with the Idea of a possible united common Will, is mine".

2.4.2. Labour Theory

Locke (1765, p.92) propounded this theory as follows:

> Though the earth and all the inferior creatures be common to all men, yet everyman has a property in his own person. This, nobody has any right to, but himself. The labour of his body and the work of his hands, we may say are properly his. Whatever then he removes out of the state that nature has provided and left it in, he hath mixed his labour with and joined to something that is his own and thereby makes it his property. It being by him removed from the common state of nature placed it in, it has by this labour something annexed to it, that excludes the common right of men.

In effect, to Locke, the investment of labour stamps the object with an element of an individual's personality in which he or she has exclusive property. So invested with the individual's personality, the object assumes a quality of such personality whereby it becomes the private property of the individual. Certainly, Locke proceeds from a premise of a utopian state of nature where an individual could be credited with the creation of an object via the investment of his or her labour. Locke's idea of transmitting part of an individual's personality to an object through expending labour upon such an object is not far removed from traditional ideas as Herskovits (1962, p.145) sees this principle as a characteristic of most African cultures:

> An individual owns the utensil or other object on which he has expended effort, whether it be mortar, a canoe or, the harvest of the field he has worked. The land he farms, though theoretically it 'belongs' to the chief as a representative of the community, is his for use; and as long as he uses it, it cannot be used by another. Regulations regarding trespass are clearly indicated in analyses of African law….. A corollary to the principle of ownership provided the sanctions needed to accomplish the transfer from communal to a more personal form of landholding, when tree crops became important. We have noted the traditional code, whereby the individual has a personal inalienable claim to those things

> for whose existence he has been responsible. Included in this category are the trees he plants in the field or fields he cultivates. The principle holds everywhere, for the fruit trees or bamboo in East Africa as it does in the Congo and the Guinea Coast. Hence one who has planted a tree must be granted access to it after he has ceased farming the plot in which he planted it, while a person who later cultivates this plot must protect such a tree from damage by fire when he burns over the field at the end of the dry season.

In some parts of Africa, immediate personal effects an individual acquires himself or herself are so closely identified with him or her that the individual is buried with them on his death on the theory that he or she would need those immediate personal effects in the world hereafter (Asante, 1975).

2.5. Origins and Development of Landed Property Rights among Ethnic Groups in SSA

Iliffe (1995) has comprehensively described the origins of ethnic groups in SSA. Iliffe's work has been extensively reviewed by Abdulai (2010), Abdulai and Antwi (2005) and West (2000) and encapsulated as follows.

> Recent linguistic and archaeological research has added considerably to our knowledge of the African past; and the earlier stages in the emergence of food-producing communities are now known to be represented by San forager-hunters and the Khoikhoi pastoralists who spoke distinctive 'click' languages and once roamed so far north of modern Kenya, but have now long been confined to the south-west extremities of the sub-continent (West 2000, p.19).

The Bantu people, from the evidence of ancestral Bantu languages seem to have originated from the region of the Niger-Benue confluence and outward migrations occurred within the period 3000-1000 B.C. Archaeological findings indicate that after this period, Bantu speaking groups moved slowly eastwards along the northern fringe of the equatorial forest belt as far as East African lakes. They were mobile pioneers, heavily reliant on foraging and hunting and later selected better land areas suited for cultivation. By 400 B.C, Bantu-speakers had carried their distinctive culture along the western edge of the equatorial forest to the lower reaches of the River Congo and then to the upper Zambesi valley. In central Africa, Congo was first inhabited by Mbuti and later joined by Bantu groups. These Bantu groups also first occupied the present day Angola, Gabon, Democratic Republic of Congo (formerly Zaire), Zambia and Central African Republic.

By the first century, Bantu and Nilotic people moved into Kenya and the former now comprise three-quarters of the population. Bantu-speaking populations migrated into Uganda and occupied most of the southern parts of the country. They came with new ideas of social and political organisation and by the fifteenth century centralised kingdoms emerged including the kingdoms of Buganda, Bunyoro-Kitare and Ankloe. Nilotic people like the Luo and Ateker entered the country from the north probably around 100 A.D. Tanzania (formerly Tanganyika) was originally inhabited by the San (Bushmen) and Hottentots but were later displaced by the Bantus and Nilotes. The Twa were the original settlers in Ruanda, the present day Rwanda, followed by the Hutus and then the Tutsis. In Urundi (Burundi), the first settlers were the Hutus, after which came the Tutsis.

Other Bantu-speaking groups moved southwards from the East African lakes region to modern Mozambique by the second century and the area of the Great Kei River around the 9th century. The early settlers in Zimbabwe were the Shona or Mashona people (around 400 A.D.); then came the Gokomere people, all Bantu speaking groups. The San were the first to settle in the modern day Namibia, South Africa, and Lesotho several years ago. Around 500 AD, they were joined by Bantu-speaking groups including the Namaqua and Damara or Berg Dama in Namibia whilst in Lesotho and South Africa they were joined by the Sotho, Zulu, Tswana, Khoikhoi and Xhosa. Around the same time, the Tswana migrated to Botswana and were the first to settle there after which followed the Shona and Ndebele. The Swazis, another Bantu-speaking group, which initially settled amongst the Zulus in the southern part South Africa were unable to match the growing Zulu strength and, therefore, moved gradually north eastwards in the 1800s; they finally settled in modern day Swaziland.

The population of the sub-region slowly and unsteadily progressed under the influence of the basic geographical controls of topography, rainfall and natural vegetation. Movement of small pioneering groups was relatively easy along the desert margins and the extensive savannah belts. Despite ecological constraints, wide spread endemic diseases, failures of rain and consequent famine, especially, in the Sahelian region, forms of peripatetic village life developed, with pottery making and eventually the smelting of copper and iron in favoured localities. Small family groups grew, multiplied and coalesced and regional trading systems emerged. In the third century, a trading settlement is known to have existed in modern Mali and a substantial town was established there by A D 400. The early settlers in Mali were Mossi and Soso followed by Mandinka people. Some members of these ethnic groups later migrated to other Sahelian areas like the present day Burkina Faso, Niger, Chad, Sudan and Mauritania.

In West Africa, the Yorubas and Hausas emerged and settled in South-West Nigeria and North-West Nigeria respectively around the 10th century. The Fulbe or Fulani pastoralists who initially settled in Senegal in the fourteenth century had spread over most of West Africa by the sixteenth century, many of who penetrated the Hausa territories. By 1471, the Anlo-Ewe had settled in South East Ghana. The population clusters in the open plain of West African savannah were being drawn together by the need for defence. Thus, social groups constructed earthen boundaries to enclose villages and kinship territories and village clusters were further coalescing into the first microstates, which in turn became the building blocks of political development. Various ethnic groups moved into Togo from all sides – the Ewe from Nigeria and Benin and Mina and Guin from Ghana.

In West African forest belt, some states emerged through conquest. In the 1790s a Fulani reformer, Usman dan Fodio led Hausa and Fulani troops in holy war (jihad), which swept through the Hausa states and Yorubaland to the south and established a Theocratic Empire based in Sokoto. Mali Empire was an Islamic Empire of the Mandinka people founded by Mansa Sundiata Keita. Other examples include those of Benin and the Akan areas of Ghana.

The preceding summary about the history of indigenous and pre-colonial settlement in the sub-region shows how attitudes towards land as both a living space and as a recognisable corporate resource originated and subsequently developed among ethnic groups. As the population increased, land became less plentiful; it therefore gained more recognition and economic importance as the essential source and basis of food security and the primary safeguard of family cohesion and continuity (West, 2000). Individual access to land rights for any purpose depended on membership of a particular community, which held the land corporately under a chief, a head family or ethnic group (West, 2000). These corporate heads thus allocated land to members of the group or non-members referred to as "strangers". Rules governing access to land were an integral part of the social structure, landownership being inseparable from social relationships and the use of land confers certain rights.

Through inheritance, the above regimes have survived up to the present time. Consequently, today the allodial interest[4] in land is vested in communities represented by chiefs and families – the families are in turn represented by family heads. From the above, the distribution of land rights is based on the socio-political system - the political history of the area from which the alliances and hierarchical relationships between lineages are derived. The leader of the land owning group is in a fiduciary position and responsible for the management of the land as a trustee on behalf of the members of the community, lineage or family. As the head, he is to account for his stewardship to the members of the community or lineage of family. Given the way indigenous landholding systems have evolved, traditional land law is by nature procedural and not documented in any form. Thus, landed property ownership is not recorded in writing but it is usually well known and recognized by the community members, particularly, by adjoining owners.

Obviously the philosophical theories that underpin land acquisition by traditional corporate bodies are the first occupancy and labour theories earlier discussed. The first occupancy theory awards ownership of an un-appropriated object to a person who occupies such object first with the intention of appropriating it to himself or herself. From the discussion on the evolution of traditional landed property ownership first occupation undoubtedly played an important role in the acquisition of landed property rights. Occupation of hitherto un-appropriated territory was one of the recognised modes of establishing sovereignty. The occupation of a territory through discovery by the first settlers was an epoch-making event, which was consecrated by later generations and solemnly invoked whenever others challenged ownership of land rights.

Where a family first occupied a place through discovery, the family became the land owning group. A chief was subsequently selected as the community grew and where he was selected from the landowning family, the family played two roles - traditional governance role and head of the land owning group. However, where the selected chief was not from the first settler family, he played only the traditional governance role.

The labour theory on the other hand invests an individual with the ownership of property into which he or she has incorporated his or her labour; that is, the investment of labour in property stamps the property with an element of a person's personality in which he or she has exclusive ownership.

[4] Allodial interest is the highest proprietary interest beyond, which there is no other superior interest. It is variously referred to as paramount, absolute, ultimate, final, or radical interest. In England for instance, the allodial interest in land is vested in the Monarch or Crown.

This theory is also perfectly applicable in the African context. Even though the first occupation principle was important, it did not exhaust the theory of land acquisition in traditional law. Wherever first occupation was admissible as a basis of ownership, the labour principle was an inevitable concomitant. Therefore, the two theories are inextricably linked. The forbears who established sovereignty by first occupation invested their labour in the process of reducing the land into their possession through clearing and hunting. The ancestors also established sovereignty by fighting and conquest and they invested their labour in wars.

Where an ethnic group (led by its chief) invaded and conquered another ethnic group, the victorious ethnic group did not differentiate between conquest and acquisition of land. The vanquished ethnic group forfeited its land that became vested in the victorious chief on trust for his ethnic group or subjects. Subsequently, the chief and his family became the land owning group as well as the royal family from where subsequent chiefs were selected for administrative and political purposes. Thus, in this regime, the chief played the two roles as already indicated above; that is, traditional governance role and head of the land owning group.

The two main methods of acquiring land by families and chiefs were therefore prior settlement and conquest. Traditionally land rights were established initially by investment of sweat and toil and subsequently by birth and kinship. Thus land rights were first of all vested in the family or ethnic group acquired via either first occupation or conquest before being redistributed to members of the landowning group (indigenes) or outsiders (strangers). It may be argued that land could have also been acquired through other means like gift but it is instructive to note that somebody might have acquired the land via these main modes before it could be gifted to another person. The two philosophical theories explain how communities represented by families and chiefs in SSA acquired the allodial interest in land.

In Ghana for example, the allodial interest in land is vested in chiefs and families/clans. In some Ghanaian communities, the families/clans are called tendamba. For South Africa, Lesotho, Botswana, Namibia, Zimbabwe, and Swaziland, land is traditionally vested in tribes headed by chiefs who control the distribution of land and allocate land to prospective acquirers for various purposes (Adams et al, 2000; Mathuba, 1999). In Ivory Coast, traditional landowners are communities and families; community or family heads therefore control the allocation of land (Delville, 2000), whilst in Niger, customarily, land is vested in canton and village chiefs (Toulmin and Quan,

2000; Delville, 2000). For Nigeria, albeit land has been nationalised, the traditional landowners are families/clans (Famoriyo, 1979).

It is the above socio-political arrangement of traditional landed property ownership systems in SSA and Africa in general that have been described as communal ownership, which do not permit individual ownership and therefore considered as an impediment to economic development and progress by various authors like Toulmin and Longbottom (2001), Ensminger (1997), Payne (1997), Fisher (1993), Naire (1984) and Posner (1981). However, according to Abdulai (2010), Abdulai and Ndekugri (2008 and 2007), Abdulai and Antwi (2005), Gyekye (1998), Migot-Adholla et al. (1991), Asante (1975), Elias (1956), and Woodman (1996 and 1985), the operation of traditional landed property ownerships systems in SSA has been completely misunderstood. The authors note that even though the systems are communal, they permit individual ownership. The exposition of Abdulai and Antwi (2005) for example, is inspirational. They use African maxims from Gyekye (1998) (some of which are cited below) to show that the individual inevitably requires the relationships and cooperation of others for most of his or her pursuits and thereby underscores the need to appreciate communal values:

- One finger cannot lift up a thing (emphasising the need for collective action).
- If one person alone scrapes the bark of a tree for use as medicine, the pieces fall to the ground (emphasising the need for mutual aid and cooperation).
- The left arm washes the right arm and the right arm washes the left arm (it is when two arms wash each other that both become clean; thus the need for inter-dependence).
- When a person descends from heaven, he or she descends into human society or human habitation (this maxim points to the fact that the human being is communal by nature and should not live in isolation from other people; it also implies that social relationships are essential for every human being).

Thus, Abdulai and Antwi opine that these maxims are an illustration of how the individual inevitably requires the relationships and cooperation of others for most of his or her pursuits and thereby underscores the need to appreciate communal values. However, the authors are quick to add that albeit a unique characteristic of the African society is the sense of community as expressed in a large body of maxims, it also fully recognises the need for individual effort in wealth creation and this is evidenced by the following popular maxims cited in Gyekye (1998, pp.47-49) that regulate African conduct:

- The clan is like a cluster of trees, which when seen from afar, appear huddled together, but would be seen to stand individually when closely approached (implying that the individual is real and his or her individuality cannot be diminished by membership in a human community).
- It is by individual effort that we can struggle for our heads (which means that individual effort is a necessary condition for fulfilling our needs and achieving our goals).
- Life is as you yourself make it (this maxim pointedly reminds an individual of his effort or her personal responsibility for the kind of life he or she leads).
- One does not fan the hot food that another may eat it or expressed in another way: nobody cracks palm kernels with his teeth for another (points to the values of initiative and responsibility – that is, one has no claim on what results from the exertion of another person's effort).

Abdulai and Antwi therefore note that with the above maxims emphasising private initiative and serving as the framework that is expected to regulate behaviour, it will be surprising for the same society to be structured in such a way as to restrict the use of private efforts in wealth creation. Linking this to landed property ownership, they rightly observe that under the communal ownership system, landed property rights are assigned to a group, but at the same time they can be exclusively assigned to private individuals who are members of the community as well as non-members. The ownership systems can therefore be best described as dual with corporate rights over landed property that has not been permanently allocated to individual members of the community like forests, waterways, grazing land etc. and individual ownership over permanently allocated property rights to individuals. It is further inspiring to note that the authors have compared the African systems of landed property ownership with what obtains in England and conclude that the origin of the African systems, the way they operate and the evolutionary trajectory that they have treaded is analogous to that of England but nobody describes the landholding system in England as communal, which does not permit private property ownership.

Based on the works of authors like Thompson (2003), Ridall (2003), MacKenzie (2002), Gillingham (1993) and Currie (1981), Abdulai and Antwi have encapsulated the historical reasons for the current position in England where the allodial interest in land is vested in the Crown as follows. Duke William of Normandy (Normandy was a separate state from England, which was ruled by a duke who owed homage to the King of France) invaded and conquered England in 1066. As far as William was concerned, there was no distinction between conquest of a country and the acquisition of land of that country. Consequently, he declared all land forfeited to him as his own. William was so pleased with the conquest and in order to reward his subjects or supporters (the Normans) who fought for him, he handed out parcels of lands them. Consistent with the notion that conquest of a country and landownership of that country were inseparable, the subjects were granted occupation and use rights to the land. They therefore held the usufructuary interest whilst the Crown remained the ultimate owner and thus held the allodial interest. The Crown is still the absolute owner of land in England. However, this absolute ownership over property acquired by families and individuals is notional, jurisdictional or ceremonial. But of course the Crown owns un-acquired landed properties like forests, mountain areas, water ways, pasture lands, etc., and therefore there are communal or group rights for such areas. Consequently, any member has the right to use such areas. The Crown is in a fiduciary position and holds the communal landed property on trust for the citizenry.

In the light of the above, Migot-Adholla et al. (1991) have aptly concluded that African traditional landed property rights systems have been incorrectly represented by most foreign anthropologists, colonial administrators, as well as nationalists' ideologues who view these systems as static polar contrasts to Western property rights systems. The systems have been completely explained via the notion of the "tragedy of the commons" (that is free for all), the thesis of Hardin (1968). However, the systems are dual in nature with both communal and individual ownership and there is a clear distinction between individual and corporate landed property rights.

A second common perception about the traditional systems of African traditional landed property ownership relates to religious connotation of landed property rights and their alienation through sale. The religious/spiritual attitude of Africans towards land has been constantly stressed in official documents and in the works of various scholars like anthropologists, sociologists and lawyers. It is, for example, argued by commentators like Mahama (2008), Hooko (2000), Posner (1981), Ollenu (1962), Manoukian

(1950) and Rattray (1923) that the most significant attachment of Africans to land is the spiritual one and that land is regarded as deities, which are worshipped and cannot be sold since deities cannot be traded. The spiritual significance of land in Africa is nicely summarised in the much celebrated words attributed to a distinguished Nigerian dignitary: "Land belongs to a vast family of whom many are dead, a few are living and a countless host are still unborn" (Cited in Asante, 1975).

As Asante (1975) rightly observes the above perception means that landownership is bound up with the cult of ancestral worship where by the departed superintend the earthly affairs of their living descendants, protecting them from natural calamities and generally, making sure that their welfare is protected but at the same time demanding in return strict compliance with ethnical prescriptions. In other words, reverence for ancestral spirits is a cardinal tenet of traditional faith and such reverence dictate the preservation of land that the living shares with the dead. Land is thus vested in an eternal entity of which the living form a small fraction – effectively, land is an ancestral trust committed to the living for the benefit of themselves and generations yet unborn and cannot be parted with.

However, a recent study on the economics of traditional landholding institutions in SSA by Abdulai (2010) has shown that the above notion stems from a lack of understanding of the basic economic principles and dynamics of the African land markets or the evolutionary trajectory that the customary landed property ownership systems have treaded in response to economic factors. The study established that once upon a time, land markets in SSA were non-existent due to the fact that land was in abundance and the issue of scarcity had not set in to prompt the creation of markets in land or trading of land. Access to land was thus through customary rules and institutions as established above. With the rapid rate of population growth together with the expansion of the global economy, however, urban land has become scarcer prompting the rapid development of land markets. Thus according to the author, land was not often sold in the past and indeed, it is still the case today in typical village communities where land is in abundance and there is very low demand. It is, however, not the case in communities where there is continuous increasing demand for land for various purposes due to population pressure. Abdulai therefore asserts that the principles of economics dictate the behaviour and actions of traditional landowners and that the value of land to people does not lie in its association with deities as in the fact that it is an asset that can be used for various purposes - it is the utilitarian concept of land, which is at play.

Abdulai's argument is corroborated with evidence from various studies like those of Quan (2000), West (2000), Bassett and Crummey (1993), Migot-Adholla et al. (1991), Downs and Reyna (1988), Feder and Noronha (1987), Noronha (1985), Raynaut (1976), Asante (1975), Boserup (1965), Hill (1963) and White (1959), which shows that whenever there was increasing demand for land in the olden days, it was traded. Hill (1963), for example, notes that in Ghana towards the end of the nineteenth century, mining possibilities attracted European attention and the successive waves of concession hunters for mining interests in gold, diamonds and other minerals influenced traditional authorities to sell land; thus, the mining boom resulted in alienation of vast expanses of land as mining concessionaires were granted in the form of long-term leases with unprecedented powers of exploitation practically amounting to transfer of ownership via sale. Hill (1963) further observes that similar consequences followed the introduction of commercial agriculture. The tremendous increase in demand for land for commercial farming resulted in a migratory movement of cocoa farmers from the congested areas of southern-eastern Ghana to more spacious lands - in the 1890s, great numbers of farmers migrated from Akuapim and Krobo states to Akim Abuakwa and purchased extensive tracts of land from chiefs (Hill, 1963).

The other perception of African customary landed property ownership systems, as earlier noted is about ownership security where it is argued that there is pure insecurity in such systems since proof of ownership is not based on any form of documentation. It is based on this notion that land registration has been promoted since the colonial era as the panacea to the problem of ownership insecurity in SSA and an examination of this issue is the main thrust of this book.

2.6. Economic Importance of Property Rights

According to Coase (1960), the property rights concept of market goods and services was normally not taken into consideration by economists in their analyses as they considered the exchange of goods and services in the market as the exchange of the physical goods. In his 1960 seminal work, Coase argued that when transactions take place in the market, it is actually property rights that are exchanged and not the physical commodities. From this premise, there are two main economic arguments in support and justification for property rights. These are the internalisation of externalities and allocation of resources arguments.

2.6.1. Internalization of Externalities

From the preceding discussions on the systems of property rights, it is clear that the primary function of property rights is the internalisation of externalities. This is therefore one of the main arguments by economists in favour of the importance and justification for property rights. In particular, the private property rights system has the advantage of internalizing these externalities at lower costs when compared with the communal property rights system as already discussed above.

2.6.2. Allocation of Resources

There is also the efficient allocation of scarce resources argument by economists in support and justification of property rights. It is well known that the paucity of resources vis-à-vis the insatiable demand for goods and services by the society is the underlying factor for the study of economics. Normally, individual members of the society are forced to make choices since all their needs cannot be satisfied due to scarce resources. However, from the discussions so far, property rights exist to organize competing uses of scarce resources in order to efficiently allocate such resources for the benefit of the society. Alchian (1967, p.370) rightly notes that without scarce resources, there is no need for property rights - the allocation of scarce resources in a society is the assignment of rights to the use of resources in a society and so the question of economics or how prices should be set is the question of how property rights should be defined and exchanged and on what terms. According Becker (1977, p.71), to be able to approximate, in operation, the idealized free market model of efficiency in allocation and justice in distribution, property rights should be well defined. Munzer (1990) also notes that all economic arrangements such us businesses and corporations may be unable to function productively until their property rights are well defined and enforced.

When the economic importance of a resource increases and the resource becomes scarce, the society begins to assert their property rights in that resource. For example, the studies of Buchanan (1975) and Demsetz (1967) show that a close relationship existed both historically and geographically between the development of private property rights in land among the various Canadian Indian ethnic groups in the Labrador Peninsula and the development of commercial fur trade several years ago. According to these studies, it was not in the interest of any person to invest in maintaining the stock of beavers due to lack of control over hunting by others. Before the commercial beaver-skin trade became established, hunting was done primarily for the purposes of food and relatively few furs were required for the hunter's family. Hunting was carried out freely without assessing the impact on other hunters. Thus, there did not exist anything resembling ownership (property rights) in the land for hunting since the resource was abundant. However, with the advent of commercial fur trade by the French, the value of the furs to the Indians increased considerably and therefore the scale of hunting rose sharply. The resource became scarce and this resulted in conflict among the separate ethnic groups. As a result of actual or potential intertribal wars, some "natural distribution" emerged that came to be recognised by all ethnic groups. A system of property rights therefore developed with the reassignment of territorial hunting grounds.

Conclusion

This chapter has discussed the property rights theory, which provides an appropriate conceptual framework for this book. The theory is used to explain the origin and development of traditional landed property rights in SSA. It is clear that the methods of land acquisition by ethnic groups and families in the past are prior settlement and conquest. Through inheritance, the ownership systems have been maintained and so today the allodial interest in land is vested in communities represented by chiefs and families – the families are in turn represented by family heads. There are various perceptions about the traditional systems of landed property ownership, one of which is the assertion that such systems of ownership are insecure and therefore land registration is promoted as the answer. Two main economic arguments are often advanced in support and justification for property rights, which are internalisation of externalities and allocation of resources arguments. Having discussed the theory of property rights, the origin and evolution of traditional landed property rights among ethnic groups in SSA, and the economic importance of property rights, a platform has been provided for subjecting the bases on which land registration is equated to ownership security to critical analyses in the next chapter.

Chapter 3

BASES OF EQUATING LAND REGISTRATION TO REAL ESTATE OWNERSHIP SECURITY

ABSTRACT

Having set the scene in chapter one and provided a theoretical framework in chapter two the main issues of the book are examined in this chapter. Thus, the meaning of ownership security and land registration has been considered. Ownership security connotes the degree of certainty that a person's ownership will be recognized by law and, particularly, by members of the society and protected when there are challenges to the ownership. It is therefore about legal and societal recognition as well as enforceability of property rights. Land registration involves a continuous recording of landed property ownership information into a central system that can easily be accessed by the public for various purposes. It also involves the continuous updating of the land register as and when necessary to ensure that it truly reflects the realities on the ground. Two land registration systems exist globally and they are deed and land title registration (Torrens) systems. The main difference between the two systems relates to the source of legal validity of ownership. In the deed registration system, legal recognition and protection of property rights emanate from the contract between the landed property grantor and grantee and not the fact of registration. However, in the Torrens system, it is the entry into the registry that gives property rights legal validity.

The bases of equating land registration to ownership security have been critically examined in this chapter in order to determine whether or not land registration can guarantee security. The examination has shown that the role that land registration is expected to play has been completely misunderstood and registration per se cannot be the panacea to the ownership insecurity problem. Thus, the actual determinants of ownership security have been defined and the right role that land registration is supposed to play has also been identified and discussed.

3.1. Introduction

The main thrust of this chapter is to examine the bases of equating land registration to ownership security. To intimate what follows, section two explains what ownership security is all about whilst section three gives an overview of land registration systems that exist globally and flowing from this, section four subjects the bases of equating registration to security to critical analysis. The actual role of land registration is defined in section five. In section six, the determinants of real estate ownership security are identified and discussed whilst section seven concludes the chapter.

3.2. An Explanation of Real Estate Ownership Security

Ownership security has been variously defined. According to Barrows and Roth (1990) ownership security is the perception of the likelihood of losing a specific right to cultivate, graze, fallow, transfer, or mortgage. As Sjaastad and Bromley (1997) rightly observe, this is actually a definition of insecurity rather than security. It is also a limited definition of insecurity since insecurity can be associated with any of the 12 rights of ownership identified by Honoré (1961) in chapter two.

Ownership security is defined by Place (2009), Kvitashvili (2004), Brasselle et al. (2001), Roth and Haase (1998), Bruce (1998), Bruce and Migot-Adholla (1994), Place et al. (1994) and Atwood (1990) in terms of breadth, duration and assurance of rights. Regarding duration, Bruce (1998), for example, explains security as the degree of confidence with which landholders expect to reap the fruits of their investments in land and thus about how long one can exercise one's rights on land. Due to the fact that it may take some time before investments begin to generate enough returns, it is argued that land rights are only secure when landholders can exercise their rights for a period of time sufficient to allow them to enjoy the fruits of their labour. Any bundle of rights that can only be exercised over a short duration is therefore regarded as insecure.

Breath (scope or size) of rights refers to the bundle of rights that one possesses and it is asserted that if a person does not possess certain property rights, which are considered key, ownership is said to be insecure because that person can only use the property in a limited way. Thus, Place (2009) and Kvitashvili (2004), for instance, are of the view that ownership becomes insecure whenever any of the following exists: (i) lack or perceived lack of some key property rights; (ii) lack of the right duration; and (iii) lack of certainty in exercising or continuous exercise of one's property rights. Also, Place et al. (1994) have observed that maximum security is achieved when an individual has rights to land on a continuous basis, free from imposition of interference from outside sources and the ability to reap the benefits of labour and capital invested in the land whether in use or on transfer to another person. Sjaastad and Bromley (2000) have explained assurance of property rights as the risk of losing property rights but that is rather a definition of insecurity. Assurance of property rights should be appropriately defined as the degree of certainty that an owner will not lose his/her property rights.

As aptly noted by Sjaastad and Bromley (2000, p.370), defining ownership security in terms of size, duration and assurance of property rights makes the concept of security intractable and thus for security to survive as a coherent concept, "....breadth of rights and duration of rights must be jettisoned, leaving only the idea of security-assurance-to do the necessary work". This is because regarding duration it cannot be a measure of security. Where a person is entitled to the exercise of, for example, rights over landed property for any given period of time, security is supposed to be measured in terms of that particular duration. Thus, if Kombian is entitled to exercise any set of rights over, for example, a parcel of land in just one day, security would have to be measured in terms of that one day and not beyond that. Duration may only determine the type of investment that can be undertaken on the land. Potential investors will acquire land for the duration that will serve the purpose for which the land is acquired. An investor who acquires land for a short duration is therefore likely to go for an investment venture that would mature within that short period and security should be measured in terms of that short period.

In terms of size, although the possession of a wide range of property rights may be described as desirable, the possession of a single right cannot amount to insecurity. Security in this instance has to be measured in terms of the right that an individual is entitled to exercise over the property; it cannot be measured in relation to what the person is not entitled. The legal maxim that "nemo dat quod non habet" (literally meaning no one can give out what he does not have) can be extended to apply here - that is, ownership security cannot be measured in terms of what one does not own. Consequently, the fact that one is entitled to the exercise of a single property right cannot amount to insecurity.

Thus, it is only assurance of property rights (the degree of certainty that an owner will not lose his property rights), which is about ownership security. It is premised on this assurance conception of security that Abdulai (2010), Abdulai et al. (2007) and FAO (2005) have defined security of ownership as the degree of certainty that a person's rights will be recognized by law and, especially, by members of the society and protected when there are challenges to such rights. Ownership security, therefore, involves two forms of validation, which are state validation by legal recognition and validation at the local level through recognition of one's rights by his/her neighbours (Toulmin and Longbottom, 2001). According to Abdulai (2010), if a person's ownership is secure, that person should be able to exercise his/her property rights peacefully or devoid of contestation and where disputes do occur, the ownership should be protected. Based on this definition, social and legal recognition of landed property rights, the absence of disputes over landed property as well as enforceability and clarity of landed property rights are all parameters of ownership security. Premised on the same conception of security, Antwi (2000), Li et al. (1998), Besley (1995), Schlager and Ostrom (1992) and Honoré (1961) have explained ownership security to be the enforceability of land rights against whom they are supposed to be enforced and immunity from expropriation.

Thus, Roth and Haase (1998) appear to be right by describing ownership security as a kind of perception held by individuals regarding their ability to exercise rights both now and in the future in a manner that is devoid of interferences from others and at the same time allows them to benefit from any investment made on the land. De Souza (1999) describes it as the perception regarding the probability of eviction. The only way an individual can exercise his rights without interference is when his entitlement to these rights are recognised by law and, especially by members of the society. The views of people on the likelihood of losing their land rights vary across persons, time and space. These perceptions are not static neither are the factors that influence them. Perception is a qualitative or subjective variable that may be difficult to measure.

Finally, there is another legal angle of ownership security, which is explained by authors like Bruce (1998). The assertion is that lawyers are more interested in how to argue cases in the law courts and a lot of the arguments are based on facts and the ability to provide hard evidence to prove one's case beyond all reasonable doubt and in the case of landed property ownership, it is achieved via land registration. Therefore according to this school of thought, the attainment of security is synonymous to the ability of landed property holders to provide documentary evidence of their ownership. Premised on this, Bloch (2003) argues that security of ownership is an objective measurable variable in that it can be quantified and proven via documentary evidence. Wannasai and Shrestha (2007), in their classification of property rights security also note that ownership is secure if landholders possess registered titles or land certificates whilst the ownership is insecure where there is no documentary evidence of ownership. Furthermore, according to Brasselle et al. (2001) it is only when land is registered and protected by legal title that maximum ownership security is afforded. It is based on this conception of security that in the developing world, the traditional landed property ownership systems, which are not based on any form of documentation, are often described as pure insecurity. Legality as noted above is a parameter of ownership security but whether it emanates from only documentation or land registration will be subjected to analysis later.

Ownership security as explained by Abdulai (2010), Abdulai et al. (2007), FAO (2005), Sjaastad and Bromley (2000), Antwi (2000), Li et al. (1998), Besley (1995), Schlager and Ostrom (1992), Honoré (1961) [and to some extent Bruce (1998)] is what has been adopted in this book since such an explanation adequately captures the right parameters on which ownership security should be based. Thus, ownership security is simply the degree of certainty that a person's ownership will be recognized by law and by members of the community, especially, adjoining owners and protected when there are challenges to it – in other words, it is about legal and societal recognition and enforceability of property rights.

3.3. Land Registration Systems

Before looking at land registration systems that are available, it is expedient to first of all explain land registration. Land registration has been described as the process of recording legally recognised rights to landed property (Griffith-Charles, 2004). This process, according to Griffith-Charles, involves the acquisition, formalisation and recording of landed property ownership data within a mechanism that continuously maintains the data to make sure it is up to date. Lamour (2002) notes that it involves the investigation, survey and registration of landed property ownership as well as creating an ongoing system that manages dealings in registered landed property.

The definition by Griffith-Charles gives the impression that an individual's rights to landed property must only be legally recognised before they get registered. Registering landed property rights that lack societal recognition even though they have legal recognition is a recipe for confusion as that can trigger the occurrence of ownership disputes since disputes over landed property can only occur because a member of the society does not recognise the ownership of another person. Societal recognition of landed property ownership should therefore be regarded a precondition for land registration. It is the only reliable variable that can prevent ownership conflicts and therefore enhance security. In the African context, legal recognition can be vulnerable and susceptible to political manipulations. Greedy politicians and dictators and their cronies may be capable of influencing the legal system to grab the most valuable landed property from the less privileged which can lead to social uprising as the underprivileged may revolt against the politicians and dictators and their cronies.

According to Atwood (1990) land registration in the African context refers to the process of authorising primary claim to landed property usually already recognised informally by the community but often ignored by the legal system. This definition implies that registration of landed property ownership is the source of formal or legal recognition but as will be discussed later it is not the case, especially under the deed registration system. Also, defining land registration in the context of Africa is problematic since it connotes the same thing irrespective of the country or continent. The principles of land registration are the same across the globe and so they are not country specific. More so, land registration was introduced in Africa by Western countries that colonised Africa based on the same principles as obtained in the Western countries.

Hogg (1920) defines land registration as a system of recording the ownership of an interest in landed property and/or landed property transactions from time to time in a public office. Abdulai (2010) and Abdulai et al. (2007) agree with this by describing land registration as a record keeping system that is intended to create a landed property ownership database for various purposes. This definition is echoed by Fiadzigbey (2000) who describes land registration as the unambiguous recording of the physical boundaries and property rights to landed property in a public register as well as the establishment and maintenance of each individual interest in the landed property.

Various authors have described land registration in different ways and albeit some of definitions are problematic, which have been pointed out above, what is common in the definitions is the fact that land registration involves a continuous recording of landed property ownership information (which includes particulars of the owner and the land concerned) into a central system that can easily be accessed by the public to inform their dealings in landed property. Another common issue in the definitions is the process of updating the landed property ownership information recorded as and when necessary to ensure that it truly reflects the realities on the ground.

Land registration is often referred to as *land titling* or *titling* in the literature on land registration and thus registered land referred to as *titled land*. However, this is a wrong terminology used by people who seem not to understand the theory of property rights, which has been explained in chapter two. As indicated in chapter two, title simply means ownership and so when somebody says he/she has title to property, it means that the person owns that property. Thus, it is erroneous to refer to land registration as *land titling* or *titling*; how can recording somebody's property ownership in a central system controlled by the state be referred to as *titling*? Indeed, it is inappropriate to use the term *land titling* or *titling* since it does not mean anything. Thus, the use of such a terminology must be consigned to the dustbin. Another commonly wrong phrase used in the literature is to the effect that *title is issued by a state institution responsible for land registration.* The implication is that *ownership* is *issued* by that state institution, which from a commonsensical perspective is meaningless. In any case, the property would have already been *owned* by somebody; just that the person would be registering his/her ownership. Also, property ownership cannot and does not emanate from land registration or the state institution charged with the responsibility of registering landed property ownership. Thus, the use of such a phrase must also be jettisoned.

In the main, there are two land registration systems that exist globally, which are deed and title registration systems. According to Deininger (2003, p.71), in the deed registration system, legally recognized and protected rights to land arise upon conclusion of an agreement or contract between the landed property grantor and grantee. The entry of the agreement or contract and its key contents into the public registry is to provide public notice of the existence of the landed property rights and challenges to such rights will be handled through civil litigation. It is thus a record of property instruments or transactions and does not provide any guarantees regarding the actual legal ownership status of the property (Asiama, 2000; Larsson, 1991).

Palmer (1998) observes that in the deed registration system, it is not the title that is registered but the evidence of title which is the instrument. This observation is, however, confusing and contradicting in that one way to prove ownership or title is by evidence and indeed if somebody has evidence of title in his/her name then it could be said that the registration of the evidence is tantamount to the registration of title. The history of the deed registration system is often traced to the Romans who introduced it in, for example, England and Wales in 397 when Britain became part of the Roman Empire, where ownership and productivity of land was recorded - it formed the basis of a land tax called *tributum soli* in England and Wales (Dark, 2000; Pemberton, 1992). Thus Britain subsequently introduced such a system of registration in the countries in SSA that it colonised (Abdulai et al., 2007). The deeds system is common in South America, parts of Asia and Africa, most parts of the United States of America and in Latin cultures in Europe, for example, France, Spain, and Italy (Enemark, 2005).

In title registration system, however, it is the entry into the registry that gives landed property rights legal validity, guaranteed by the state – all entries in the register are *prima facie* evidence of the actual legal status of the landed property (Deininger, 2003, p.71). The state guarantees the accuracy of the data entered in the title register and in some jurisdictions, the state indemnifies or pays compensation (from an indemnity fund set up) to owners who suffer any loss due to negligence, mistakes, errors and omissions from the registration system as well as fraud unless the owners contributed substantially to the occurrence of these events. Title registration involves all the features of a deed registration system and therefore any change in ownership of landed property, which may arise from sales is captured by the title register (Hogg, 1920). Therefore there must always be a continuous effort to keep the register up to date. Where the title register fails to capture any changes in landed property ownership, the new holders of the property may not be legally recognised as such at least in principle. It may thus be possible in such instances for previously registered owners to still deal with the landed property as if they had not transferred the property. However, in most developing countries including SSA, updating the register remains a theory that is difficult to implement (Torhonen, 2004).

Land title registration is based on the Torrens system, which has been described in Abbott (2005) and Clay County Recorder (2004). The Torrens system was originally a ship registration system - a method used to record ownership rights in ships as used by the British Ship Registry. In the ship registration system, each ship owner is assigned a certificate that includes information about the ship. When a vessel is sold, the seller surrenders the certificate for cancellation. The ship is then registered in the name of the new owner and a new certificate is issued to him/her. In this way, a reliable ship ownership information system is created.

Sir Robert Richard Torrens (1814-1884), an Irish emigrant to Australia and a land law reformer extended the above idea to land. In 1858, he devised a system of land registration for Australia based on the ship registration system. Because Sir Torrens was the progenitor of the idea in terms of land, it was named after him as the Torrens system, which explains why the land title registration system is also often referred to as the Torrens system. He became the first Registrar of Land Deeds in Australia.

Under the system, land title cannot pass and no encumbrance can be enforced, unless it is noted in a land register. The actual transfer of land title is evidenced by registration - the cancellation of an old title certificate and the issuing of a new certificate in the name of the new proprietor by the Registrar of Titles. The system also provides a means of recording in a systematic fashion, all liens (public or private), court orders, easements, restrictions, encumbrances, leases and rights of third parties (especially those in possession) that affect every recorded parcel of land. As a rule any item that is not recorded and thereby noted on the title certificate is not binding on a *bona fide* purchaser of registered land albeit in some jurisdictions, there are exceptions in the case of minor interests like short-term leases. The purpose of the system as Sir Torrens himself aptly puts it is to simplify landed property transfer. Sir Torrens was looking for five qualities when he introduced land title registration - reliability, simplicity, low cost, speed, and suitability. In Australia, even though, the Torrens system has been adopted in every State, it is by no means uniform as there are significant differences between the States on such matters as forms of co-ownership, the recognition of claims based on adverse possession, the division between the requirements for registration of formal and informal leases, and the recognition of implied easements and restrictive covenants.

The Torrens system is premised on three principles, which are mirror, curtain and guarantee or insurance principles (Zevenbergen, 2002). The mirror principle is where the register acts literally as a mirror reflecting accurately the reality regarding ownership of landed property rights. Thus an inspection of the register should reveal the identity of the landed property owner, nature of the ownership, any limitations on such ownership and any rights enjoyed by other persons over the landed property (Lawrance, 1980). The mirror principle must therefore rely heavily on the ability of the authorities involved in land registration to continuously update the register. Failure to capture events such as landed property transfers as and when they occur will imply that at any point in time the true state of landed property ownership will be different from that portrayed by the register. It should be noted that the operation of the mirror principle in practice is limited by the presence of overriding interests – these are third party property rights of great importance such that they bind a purchaser or the holder of title whether or not he/she has knowledge of them and even if they are not mentioned in the register; an example being an easement (Abdulai, 2010). The title registration system is commonly used in Central European countries like Germany, Austria and Switzerland (Enemark, 2005).

The curtain principle according to Zevenbergen (2002) and Henssen (1995) takes away the need to go beyond the register in search for historical information on landed property ownership. This implies that the register basically provides the public with landed property ownership data at every point in time at least in theory and once this data is guaranteed to be accurate there will be no need to trace the historical roots of title to any property. Premised on this principle, where the landed property is subject to a trust, only the legal title is shown on the register and there is no need to go behind the register to search for equitable interests. Thus a purchaser who wishes to buy property that is subject to a trust needs to be concerned with only the legal title held by the trustees. All equitable interests are kept off the title as the beneficiaries will be overreached on sale; that is, equitable interests will be converted to cash upon the sale of the landed property and the trustees will hold the purchase money on trust for the equitable owners.

Under the guarantee or insurance principle, the state guarantees the accuracy of any registered landed property ownership and thus the register is conclusive evidence of ownership (Zevenbergen, 2002; McLaughlin and Williamson, 1985). It is based on this principle that as earlier indicated, compensation is payable from public funds to registered proprietors who are deprived of their title or are otherwise prejudiced by the operation of the scheme or suffer any losses by reason of the conclusive nature of the register. Registered landed property rights are said to be given priority over unregistered rights in terms of claim right (Simpson, 1976). However, in instances where several registered rights exist or where there is double transfer, priority may be established based on the principles race and notice (Zevenbergen, 2002). By the race principle, the winner of the race to the registry as evidenced by the order in which the instruments appear on the register is given priority over everyone else. However, under the notice principle, more attention appears to be directed towards the provision of notice of an interest in the property.

What this means is that, for instance, if Kombian registers his interest in landed property first before Konlan, under the race principle, Kombian has the prior claim right over Konlan. However, under the notice principle if the fact of Kombian's registration is not regarded as sufficient notice, then Konlan may have the prior claim right if his registration is considered sufficient notice to the public even though he registered his interest at a much later date than Kombian. The notice principle thus appears to emphasise on the provision of sufficient public notice of various interests in landed property rather than merely recording them. Though Kombian might have registered his interest first, if it was not sufficient notice, he loses his prior claim right. This is because purchasers of such landed property could always plead bona fide purchasers for value without notice. In principle, all bona fide purchasers for value without appropriate notice are given first claim rights. The first to provide sufficient notice of a particular interest obtains priority over all others.

Hogg (1920) in an attempt to differentiate between the deed and title registration systems notes their close similarity and the difficulty in distinguishing them but argues that the presence of a statutory provision of title warranty in the title registration system is the single most important distinguishing feature between the two systems. It is important to note that Hogg has completely down played one other equally critical distinguishing feature between the two systems, which is source of legal validity - whilst the land title registration system is a source of legal validity of ownership, the deed registration system is not. Therefore there are two important factors that differentiate one registration system from the other and that is even from a theoretic perspective. According to Zevenbergen (2002), under the title registration systems in countries like Germany, Sweden and Denmark there are no state guarantees as protection for registrants is only derived from "public faith". Consequently, from a practical perspective, the main difference between the two registration systems is rather the source of ownership legality. Thus, practically, the deeds registration system can be appropriately described as the recording of mere legal facts (transactions that have taken place between landed property grantors and grantees) whereas land title registration system is about the recording of legal consequences of transactions.

In terms of the methods of land registration, it can be compulsory or voluntary (Larsson, 1991) and it can also be systematic or sporadic

(Zevenbergen, 2002). In the compulsory land registration system, the relevant laws make registration compulsory upon the occurrence of certain events. The current legislation governing land registration in England and Wales (Land Registration Act 2002) is a perfect example that can be used to illustrate the difference between compulsory and voluntary registration since both systems operate concurrently. Under Act 2002 there are trigger events that make registration of title compulsory within two months even though an extension could be obtained on application depending on the circumstances. These events include: (a) a transfer of freehold interest (previously registered or unregistered) via sale or by way of gift; (c) a vesting assent; (c) a grant of a leasehold interest for more than seven years for valuable consideration or other consideration or by way of gift; (d) an assignment of a leasehold interest with more than seven unexpired for valuable consideration or other consideration or by way of gift; and (e) a deed of mortgage. Where the transaction is not registered within the required period, it becomes void. Thus, in the case of transfer by sale for instance, where the disposition is not registered within two months, the interest reverts to the transferor, who then holds the interest on trust for the intended purchaser. When the legal interest remains vested in the transferor and there is any subsequent transaction regarding the interest, which is registrable and is registered before the first transferee applies for registration after the mandatory period has elapsed, the first registered interest has priority or takes precedence over the interest of the first transferee.

Compulsory land registration was introduced in England and Wales in 1990 and so if for example Konlan owned a landed property that was not registered before 1990 and since then Konlan has remained the owner of the property, it is not obligatory for him to register his title providing none of the above trigger events has occurred on his landed property. However, Konlan can apply voluntarily to register his title to the property for the first time. There is thus a creeping registration and currently, HM Land Registry is offering 25% discount on the cost of registration as an incentive for owners to voluntarily register their landed property titles (HM Land Registry, 2011). Under Act 2002, owners of the following interests can apply to register voluntarily: freehold; leasehold; rent charge; franchise (a right granted by the Crown entitling the holder to for example hold a fair or market and therefore receive rents from the stall holders of take tolls from traffic passing over a bridge; and profits a prendre in gross. The Act also enables Crown land (demesne land) to be registered voluntarily.

Regarding systematic and sporadic registration systems, Janczyk (1979) has explained the difference between the two as follows. In the sporadic registration system, normally, an official declaration of an area as a registration district is made by the State after the necessary infrastructure has been put in place. Once this is done the public is expected to apply for registration and parcels of land to be registered are surveyed individually. Apart from the above initial action, the State really does not do much. The assumption here it is that the public understands the value of registration and will patronise it willingly. However, this does not often happen in reality, especially where people are reasonably happy with any previous systems (Larsson, 1991). Sporadic registration is thus for all intents and purposes voluntary registration and as Larsson aptly notes, such a registration system takes a long time to complete the register.

Under systematic registration, once an area is declared a registration zone, it is followed by the preparation of a cadastral map of the whole registration zone. Owners of land must indicate their land boundaries in this process as well as indicate the exact rights they wish to claim with the relevant supporting written evidence or oral evidence backed by sworn statements. In the systematic system, registration starts only in one part of the country and gradually extends to other parts as previously declared registration zones are covered. Systematic registration is normally compulsory. In a compulsory systematic registration system, landowners are not required to submit applications for their land to be registered. The State simply registers all lands even though the owners may be asked to pay the necessary fees (Larsson, 1991). This is said to be prevalent in areas where land reforms are aimed at transferring public lands to private individuals or vice versa. Registration under this system is aided by cadastral survey of one area after the other. This system according to Larsson, involves low cost of registration as the huge initial cost is mostly borne by the State. This system appears to require a high level of commitment on the part of the State, especially in terms of resources. Regarding a compulsory sporadic registration system, registration is obligatory only when certain events are triggered as explained above. Obviously, it is an amalgam of compulsory and voluntary registration and thus England and Wales operate the compulsory sporadic registration system.

3.4. WHY LAND REGISTRATION IS EQUATED TO OWNERSHIP SECURITY

There are three main dimensions to the argument that land registration is the answer to insecurity of landed property rights or guarantees landed property ownership security, which are subjected to critical analyses in the following sections.

3.4.1. Title Warranty Provided by the State

One basis of equating land registration to ownership security relate to the title warranty provided by the state under the Torrens system. Commentators like MacGee (2006), Jacoby and Minten (2005) and Simpson (1984) equate registration to security based on such warranty. Simpson, for example, notes that because of such guarantee, title registration makes landed property ownership indefeasible or unimpeachable. Indeed, the land title registration laws of some countries specifically state that title registration is conclusive evidence of ownership and that it makes title indefeasible. In Ghana, for instance, Section 18 of the title registration legislation [Land Title Registration Law 1986 (PNDCL 152)] provides that the title register is conclusive evidence of title to all landed property and interest in it and therefore indefeasible, which is reinforced in Section 43 of same law.

Although it is argued that the Torrens system guarantees ownership security because of the title warranty provided by the state, it is obvious that the guarantee is provided by the state and not the registration system per se. Thus the state could decide not to provide that guarantee as in the case of the deed registration system. Indeed, it is possible for the state to guarantee title without any form of registration. Therefore granted that the state warranty can potently protect ownership, it is clear that land registration by itself cannot provide that protection since it actually emanates from the state; if the registration system could provide that warranty there will be no need for the state to provide it.

It is also significant to note that in some jurisdictions like Germany, Sweden and Denmark as earlier noted above, no state warranties are provided under the Torrens system and so protection for registrants is only derived from "public faith" just like the deed registration system. Indeed, in jurisdictions like the UK and USA where the state provides guarantees, the evidence from case law as provided in chapter one shows that owners of registered land under the Torrens system have lost their landed property ownership via civil litigation. This means that in such jurisdictions, the protection is not automatic and there are instances where the state guarantee or warranty would not be forthcoming.

3.4.2. Publicity Function of Land Registration

The argument of some commentators that land registration guarantees security is premised on the publicity function of land registration described supra. For instance, according to Scott (1981) during the earliest days of colonization, there was a clear understanding of the essential role of "Public Record" as a means of establishing security of private interests in landholdings. Larsson (1991) on his part argues that the publicity function of land registration prevents the occurrence of land disputes, which significantly reduces the work of state sponsored courts.

However, the above argument is unconvincing. This is because publicity of land ownership and transactions is about making people aware of somebody's ownership or landed property transactions but that is completely different from the society recognizing one's ownership and allowing the owner to exercise his or her landed property rights peacefully as well as the legal recognition of such rights, which is what ownership security is all about.

Even though, premised on this publication function of land registration, Larsson argues that land registration prevents the occurrence of disputes on registered land, the evidence adduced in various studies cited earlier in chapter one sharply debunks such an argument. Indeed, in a human society, land disputes are bound to occur and so it is unimaginable for anybody to argue that land registration prevents the occurrence of disputes.

3.4.3. Legality of Ownership

Regarding the legal conception of ownership security, under the fundamental principles of the deed registration system, societal and legal recognition of ownership and its protection arise upon conclusion of the agreement between the landed property grantor and grantee. Ownership security does not therefore emanate from the fact of registration. Entry of the key contents of the agreement into the public registry is only to provide public notice of the existence of the landed property rights and challenges to such rights will be handled through civil litigation. This clearly shows that the deed registration system does not play a role in the resolution of ownership disputes in the law courts let alone to guarantee security. Obviously, in resolving landed property disputes, the courts would of necessity rely on the contract or agreement that is entered into between the property grantor and grantee and not the fact of registration.

Admittedly, premised on the theoretical principles that underpin the Torrens system, it constitutes evidence of legal ownership. It can therefore be argued that it plays a role in the resolution of disputes in state sponsored courts as registered land title can be tended as evidence of legal ownership. Consequently, the system may be described as a determinant of security. Notwithstanding this, it has to be noted that the Torrens system "being a determinant of security" cannot in any way be equated to "guaranteeing security" – these are completely two different things. If for example, "X contributes to the occurrence of event Y or X is one of the determinants of event Y" it is not the same as saying that "X guarantees the occurrence of an event Y". The former means that X is one of the factors that would make event Y to occur; in effect, there are other factors whilst the latter means that the occurrence of event Y is dependent on only X. The thrust of this book is, however, about the latter and not the former. If the Torrens system were to guarantee security, then no registered owner of landed property under such a system can lose his ownership but as already established from case law that is not the case.

Also, title registration is not the only source of legal ownership. In most jurisdictions in Africa, although proof of traditional landed property ownership is not based on registration or any form of documentation, such ownership is recognised by their legal systems. In Ghana, for instance, traditional landed property ownership systems are recognised by the 1992 Constitution, the supreme law of the country and the Conveyancing Decree of 1973 (NRCD 175) and therefore admissible in state sponsored courts as evidence of legal ownership in times of challenges (Abdulai et al., 2007). This recognition in Ghana dates back to the colonial era when Native Courts were established in 1925. Similarly, in Nigeria despite the nationalisation of land under the Land Use Decree of 1978, traditional landed property rights are recognised by the state sponsored courts (Ikejiofor et al., 2004) whilst in Mozambique, customary landed property rights are recognised and protected regardless of whether they have been registered or not (Cotula et al., 2006).

Consequently, if the Torrens system is a determinant of security and it is equated to guaranteeing security, then the customary landed property ownership systems equally guarantee security as they are socially and legally recognised. Thus, from the legal conception of security, land registration is not needed in the customary landed property sector for security to be established. It is therefore astounding that the customary landed property ownership systems are considered to be purely insecure albeit they are legally recognised; however, regarding the Torrens system, the argument is that it guarantees security because it is a source of legal ownership.

Allied to the legal conception of security is the issue of documentary evidence of ownership. Customary landed property rights are described as purely insecure because ownership is not documented. Admittedly, when ownership is documented, it is normally easy to prove in the event of occurrence of disputes over it. However, this does not in any way imply that ownership security is guaranteed. In resolving disputes in state sponsored courts, what has to be established beyond reasonable doubt is the truth about who actually owns the property to ensure that there is no miscarriage of justice - delivery of judgements is not merely contingent upon proof of documentary evidence of ownership or registered ownership. Indeed, documents are not sacrosanct as they can be phony documents and so the mere fact that ownership is evidenced by a document does not mean that the evidence is conclusive. It is also argued as if documentation is achieved via only land registration. If for the sake of argument it is even assumed that documentation guarantees security, there can be documentation without land registration and so it is surprising that the focus is on land registration. It is common knowledge that there is documentary evidence of various things but such evidence is not registered or recorded in a central system controlled by the state.

Furthermore, physical possession and occupation as evidence of ownership in the customary landed property sector is legally recognised albeit it is not based on documentation. The potency of this form of evidence is amply demonstrated by the operation of limitation or prescription laws. Under such laws, a true owner of landed property can be dispossessed of his/her property via a reasonable period of occupation by a squatter. In Ghana, under the Limitation Decree of 1972 (NRCD 54), a trespasser dispossesses the true owner of landed property if the trespasser occupies the property for 12 years and within such period, the true owner fails to assert his ownership. At the end of the prescription period, the true owner loses his/her ownership and the right to sue is extinguished. Even where the property has been registered by the true owner, he/she still forfeits the property.

Similarly, under the French Civil Code, the prescription period is 20 years where the true owner is resident outside the territory in which the landed property is located; if the true owner lives within the territory where the property is located, the limitation period is 10 years. Also, in England and Wales, the relevant law is the Limitation Act (1980) and the limitation period is 12 and 10 years for unregistered and registered land respectively. It is not only the customary evidence of landed property ownership that is legally recognised even though it is not based on documentation. It is common knowledge that in other cases, oral evidence from witnesses is admissible in the state sponsored courts as sufficient proof of one's case and it is possible for people without documentary proof of evidence to obtain judgement in their favour.

Based on the preceding discourse, does it mean that land registration is not needed or it does not serve any purpose in the economies of nations and should therefore be jettisoned? The answer to the question is a big "NO" and this is discussed in the next section.

3.5. Role of Land Registration

There is no doubting the role that landed property and its registration play in the development of a nation but such role has been completely misunderstood. Although landed property, funds, equity, life insurance and other types of investments can be used as additional collateral for investment loans (apart from income earning capacity or income level of the investor, which is used to amortize the loan and also serves as a form of security), landed property remains the dominant one and is therefore normally required for mortgage purposes.

The importance of mortgaging one's landed property to banking institutions cannot be over-emphasised from the perspective of both the mortgagor and the mortgagee. This is because collateral arrangements shift the risks of loan loss from the mortgagee to the mortgagor. In the event of default on the part of the mortgagor, it will trigger the loss of his/her mortgaged landed property. Thus for the mortgagee, the collateral provides additional form of protection or insurance against the loss of the loan since the law normally makes provision for the mortgage to be foreclosed where the mortgagor defaults. At the same time, the prospect of losing one's landed property is an incentive for the mortgagor to be committed regarding the repayment of the loan granted.

The pledging of landed property, accompanied by registration of ownership and mortgage transactions tremendously overcomes the problems of asymmetrical information and moral hazard. When information is recorded in a central system, which is accessible to the public, it makes it easy for such data to be accessed for various purposes and therefore the importance of any recording keeping system cannot be overemphasized. Any form of a record keeping system facilitates activities or transactions, thereby reducing transaction costs. Land registration is simply a record keeping system and it is this same purpose that it serves. Land registration creates a landed property ownership database, which facilitates landed property transactions, thereby, reducing transactions costs; the ownership database, for example, facilitates title searches for mortgage purposes as ownership details can easily be accessed.

Larsson (1991) alludes to the above purpose when he explains two basic historical reasons for landownership record keeping - the need for: (a) the state to know all parcels of land for taxation or other fees; and (b) prospective land purchasers to get publicity for their acquisition of land. It is the same purpose that de Soto (2000) refers to when he emphasises the role of land registration in facilitating communication, information sharing, networking and transactions. Land registration and land markets are inextricably linked - land registration facilitates the land transfer process and subsequently ensures the transparency of transactions and further provides records for land market operations (Farvacque and McAuslan, 1992). According to Larsson (1991) and Dowson and Sheppard (1956) the earliest evidence of official landownership record keeping for purposes of taxation and other services dates as far back as 3000 BC in ancient Egypt where such records were kept in the royal registry.

Landownership record keeping for, particularly, taxation purpose has been in existence since society adopted sedimentary agriculture as evidenced by the Babylonians when they occupied the lands between the Tigris and the Euphrates and the Egyptians cultivated the fertile Nile regions (Dale and McLaughlin, 1989). Similarly, for taxation purpose, land registration was introduced in ancient Rome during the 3rd Century, in China around 700 AD based on crop yields, in South India around 1000 AD (Larsson, 1991) and in England and Wales 1086 via the famous Domesday survey, which was ordered by William the Conqueror (Plucknett, 2007). King Gustav of Sweden in 1540 also ordered the registration of all farms for taxation purpose (Larsson, 1991). Toulmin (2008) observes that land registration provides governments with information on landownership and plot sizes as well as the foundation for a property tax system.

Generally, in the absence of a land registration system, legal experts are often commissioned to conduct searches to trace the root of title in landed property transactions in order to verify that the property is not subject to any undisclosed obligations, which is normally a long process, time consuming and expensive. In the England and Wales, for example, where landed property is not registered and it is to be traded, the law requires that the root of title has to be investigated 15 years back, which used to be 30 years before 1970 and in the case of France it is 30 years. In the African context, in the absence of land registration or a landed property ownership database, the only way of verifying landed property ownership information provided by owners is to go around asking members of the communities in which the properties are located; this is obviously a herculean task albeit not impossible. Thus any land registration system significantly enhances the smooth operation of landed property markets as well as reduces transaction costs.

Other types of registration are used here to illustrate the above important purpose and to show that any record keeping system per se cannot guarantee ownership security. When somebody gives birth and registers the child at the Births Registry and a birth certificate is issued, the registration or birth certificate does not change the personality, intelligence or sex of the child. It does not also protect or secure the child. An advantage of the birth registration is that if anyone wants to know the number of children who were born in a particular year, he/she does not have to go about asking parents to know those who gave birth in that particular year, which a herculean task (even though not impossible). He/she would simply go to the Births Registry to get that information. Furthermore, when somebody buys a car and registers it, the registration does not guarantee the security of ownership or make the car ownership indefeasible since the car can be stolen or lost through accident. The only way to protect one's car in these circumstances is to insure the car against theft or accident. It may be argued that a car will have to be registered before insurance can be done but the fact that insurance has to be taken amply demonstrates that the fact of car registration per se cannot guarantee security of ownership. Otherwise nobody would register a car at a cost in some countries and still take insurance at an additional cost if registration can do the job of insurance. Similarly, in jurisdictions where car registration is free, nobody would register a car and still take insurance at a cost when registration, which is free can do the job of insurance.

In terms of mortgage registration, the common law position is that if a mortgage transaction is not registered and the mortgagor clandestinely transfers the mortgaged property via sale to a bona fide purchaser for value who is unaware of the existence of the mortgage transaction, the mortgage as an encumbrance will not be binding on such a purchaser. However, if the mortgage transaction is registered, the purchaser cannot defend himself/herself on the basis that he is a bona fide purchaser for value without notice since the existence of the mortgage will be a public record and based on the principle of caveat emptor, it will be his/her responsibility to check the public records. Thus the registration of mortgage transactions protects lenders or banking institutions from the activities of unscrupulous mortgagors as it makes it impossible for any purchaser of mortgaged landed property to plead bona fide purchaser for value without notice. Therefore apart from the interest charged on loans, registration of mortgages provides an additional incentive for banks to grant investment loans. What should then be the determinants of ownership security?

3.6. Determinants of Real Estate Ownership Security

The actual determinants of ownership security are social and legal recognition of landed property rights, availability of landed property rights dispute resolution and enforcement institutions, clear boundary demarcation of land property, and property ownership (title) insurance, which are discussed in the following sub-sections.

3.6.1. Societal and Legal Recognition of Landed Property Rights

Recognition of property rights by the legal system and most especially by the society at large is a critical determinant of ownership security. As Becker (1977, p.21) aptly observes, if Kombian has the right to possess property, not only that others do not have the right to the property, but they have a duty not to interfere with the possession of Kombian – perhaps even to see to it that the property is restored to Kombian when lost. Indeed, this factor is not only applicable to landed property but to any other form of asset. When there is a contestation over the ownership of any form of asset, it is because one party does not recognise the ownership of the other party. Once the property rights held by someone are recognized and respected by members of the society, such rights become legitimate in the eyes of the society and are easily enforced.

It is probably based on the above that Deininger (2003) has observed that in the traditional landed property ownership systems, legal recognition of exiting rights and institutions, subject to minimum conditions, is generally more effective than premature attempts at establishing formalized structures - legal recognition of traditional landed property rights and the establishment of internal rules and mechanisms for conflict resolution greatly enhance security of landed property rights. As already indicated one's property rights need not be documented or registered before they are socially and legally recognised.

3.6.2. Availability of Landed Property Rights Dispute Resolution and Enforcement Institutions

Even though recognition and respect of an individual's landed property rights is important for the enforcement of property rights, the chances that such rights would be violated cannot still be ruled out in a human society. However, if the rights were violated, the dispute would have to be resolved and therefore there is the need for appropriate dispute resolution and enforcement institutions that can authoritatively interpret property rights and resolve disputes, so as to enforce the property rights. Thus the availability of appropriate dispute resolution institutions is another critical determinant of ownership security. The availability of appropriate institutions for landed property rights dispute resolution and accessibility to such institutions provide enormous returns in terms of certainty and security of property rights - new technologies such as computerised landed property information systems can help put in place publicly accessible property ownership records, but are not a substitute for legitimate process to adjudicate landed property rights disputes (Cotula et al., 2006).

It is well documented that there are two main types of dispute resolution approaches: the formal system and informal system, which is an alternative dispute resolution approach. Where the legitimacy of such dispute resolution systems is well established, then parties to any landed property ownership dispute can seek redress from them with the assurance that whatever decisions are arrived at are deemed appropriate and can be effectively enforced. When there are institutions that can interpret landed property rights in an authoritative manner and people understand the way they work and are willing to abide by whatever decisions they make, landed property related disputes are amenable to resolution.

3.6.3. Clear Landed Property Boundary Demarcation

Landed property boundaries need to be clearly defined and easily identified by the community, especially, by adjoining owners. When boundaries are clearly defined, boundary disputes would be minimal. Accurate and precise well-defined boundaries are easier to enforce and cost less to protect as they are easily observable by other community members. Thus, the precision with which boundaries are defined and demarcated is an important determinant of ownership security.

As established by Abdulai (2010) generally land boundaries, for example, in the traditional land sector in SSA are shown on the ground by a combination of streams/rivers, old trees/hedges, valleys, hills and paths. Certainly, this has sustainability problems as, for instance, trees can perish and paths can vanish. The solution to this problem requires a scientific way of demarcating land boundaries – land surveying and pillaring to produce permanent boundary lines and maps or plans. This ensures that there is documentation of the boundaries, but doing this does not necessarily require land registration. The word "documentation" and "registration" are often used interchangeably and this seems to be the case with Larsson (1991) when he observes that the best way to clarify land boundaries is to register land. This in turn, he argues leads to less litigation and less work for the courts. However, it is misleading to use the words interchangeably. Land can be surveyed and maps produced (an effective tool that clarifies land boundaries), which is a form of documentation without registering the land.

3.6.4. Real Estate Ownership Insurance

A mechanism that can effectively address insecurity of property rights is title insurance. Title insurance is a contractual arrangement whereby the insurer indemnifies a landed property owner if he/she loses the insured property. The history of title insurance traces to the USA where the first title insurance company was formed in 1876 after the famous Pennsylvania case of Watson *v*. Muirhead in 1868 (cited in Moody, 2005). Muirhead lost his registered landed property due to an outstanding prior lien that a conveyancer had missed. He then sued the conveyancer but lost the case. This landmark decision of the Supreme Court triggered the concept of title insurance. It is different from other property related insurance like insuring the contents of a building or the physical property against calamities like fire. In title insurance, it is the bundle of rights exercisable over the property (that is, the interest in the property), which is insured.

Title insurance provides guarantees in landed property transactions by protecting the owner or lender against defective ownership or title, which results from problems like unknown recorded liens, forgeries, improperly delivered title deeds, defects in public records and incompetent grantors (Arrunada, 2001). Moody (2005) echoes this point when he notes that it provides for a more efficient closing for buyers, sellers and lenders by protecting these parties from ownership discrepancies and allowing a smooth transition of mortgage assets from the primary market to the secondary market; that is, the function of title insurance is to insure the integrity of landed property ownership, which in turn, increases the liquidity of property ownership thereby smoothing ownership transfer.

Title insurers spend a lot on title searches and identification of defects and curing such defects as they pay in claims (Sirmans and Dumm, 2006). Obviously, securing landed property ownership requires an identification of the causes of insecurity and addressing them and that is exactly what title insurers spend most of their resources and time doing. Thus, it focuses more on loss prevention rather than loss reimbursement (Moody, 2003) even though the insurer will indemnify the titleholder where the defects ultimately result in loss of ownership. Title insurance per se does not necessarily prevent the loss of landed property ownership but where it does occur the insurance ensures that the insured is reinstated via the payment of indemnity and, thus, technically there is no loss. It is therefore a tool that potently deals with landed property ownership insecurity for smooth transactions and investment.

According to Arrunada (2001) title insurance is present in about 85% of America's residential sale transactions irrespective of land registration. Due to its huge protections and benefits, it is currently adopted in nearly 60 countries (apart from America), with Canada being the second largest country for title insurance after America (Calder et al., 2004). Whilst recognizing the effectiveness of title insurance in protecting ownership, many consumers in the USA believe that the cost of the insurance in terms of premium payment is high (Ford, 1982). Thus, the problem with title insurance could be the cost involved but it is definitely a tool that effectively protects and guarantees landed property ownership.

The emergence of title insurance and its extensive practice in countries like the USA and Canada is in recognition of the fact that land registration is not the answer to ownership insecurity. In the USA and Canada, for example, both the deed and title registration systems operate. In Canada, it is title registration that is predominantly used. If it is land registration that guarantees security why is it that in the USA and Canada the owners of landed property registered under the deed or title registration systems still insure ownership/title? Why should a landed property owner pay to register his property and still incur an extra cost (which is known to be high) to insure ownership for protection if indeed, registration already does the job?

The guarantee that is supposed to be provided by the state under the title registration or Torrens system could serve the same insurance purpose advocated for here if the state actually indemnifies owners of registered landed property in situations where they lose their properties via civil litigation or any other means. Granted that this was the case, as earlier explained, it is the state that is providing the guarantee or insurance and not land registration per se; it is possible for the state not to provide that warranty as in the case of the deed registration system. Also in some jurisdictions the state does not provide it even under the Torrens system.

Conclusion

The meaning of landed property ownership security, land registration systems and their theoretical underpinnings as well as the bases of equating land registration to ownership security have been examined in this chapter in order to determine whether or not land registration can guarantee security. The discussion has shown that land registration by itself cannot be the panacea to the ownership insecurity problem, implying that land registration has been made to perform the wrong purpose. Thus, the right role that land registration plays has been identified and the actual determinants of ownership security are defined.

Chapter 4

SUMMARY AND POLICY IMPLICATIONS

4.1. SUMMARY

This book has critically examined the theoretical underpinnings of land registration systems in order to provide more insights as to why land registration cannot guarantee real estate ownership security. To comprehensively handle this, issues of land registration, ownership security, accessibility to formal credit and investment for wealth creation and development have been considered. To set the tone for the book, chapter one examines studies on the relationship that exists between land registration and ownership security. It has been established that land registration may contribute to real estate ownership security in some cases but that does not mean that it guarantees ownership security, which is the thrust of this book. Indeed, in some circumstances, it can constitute a source of ownership insecurity.

Chapter one has also assessed the impact of land registration and ownership security on access to formal credit for investment in landed property related activities. Regarding the link between ownership security and investment, it is admitted that security can be a determinant of investment. However, an examination of the theoretical model that links ownership security (in a manner to suggest that once there is security, investment would automatically happen) bespeaks that the importance of security has been over-emphasized in the literature. Even though security can enhance an individual's willingness to invest in landed property related activities, there are other equally important factors like financial capability as well as conduciveness of the environment for investment activities. It is a combination of these factors that can sufficiently motivate an individual to invest. Thus in terms of agricultural activities particularly, the demand and supply side effects of the model discussed in this chapter would not be realisable in SSA due to the existence of poverty in pandemic proportions, the absence of an enabling agricultural investment climate and the deprived nature of rural communities where most farmers reside.

In terms of the relationship between land registration and access to formal capital for investment, the discussion in the chapter has shown that there are various critical factors that actually determine the ability of landed property owners to use their property as collateral to access investment loans from financial institutions and it is not about land registration. Of course, based on the internal rules and regulations of a particular banking institution, it is possible that the only evidence of landed property ownership acceptable for mortgage purposes will be a registered title. Thus on this premise, land registration becomes just one of the several variables. However, if there are many variables that will make something to occur, it will be very erroneous and unsustainable for anybody to argue that the occurrence of that thing is dependent on only one of the several variables. However, that is exactly the argument that is made regarding the relationship between land registration and accessibility to formal credit.

The evidence adduced in chapter one shows that in the main, the prerequisites for access to formal credit are decided by financial institutions. Therefore even with registration, it is possible for landed property not to be accepted by banks as collateral and without registration landed property can also be accepted as collateral. Furthermore, financial institutions can grant loans for business or investment without collateral in the form of landed property. It is even common knowledge that international banks and other financial institutions as well as advanced countries have been granting huge loans to the developing world but the granting of such loans is not based on land registration. So it is not about land registration but rather about the internal rules and regulations of financial institutions in terms of granting loans. "He who pays the piper calls the tune" and that is exactly what the financial institutions do. Registration of landed property ownership does not automatically entitle owners to credit from financial institutions.

Indeed, people can hold registered titles but are not interested in accessing loans from the financial institutions using their registered landed property. Thus the fact of landed property registration does not automatically incentivise property owners to obtain formal credit for investment and wealth creation, neither does it guarantee accessibility to formal credit by the poor. It is also argued as if financial institutions are the only source of capital for investment purposes. Investment capital can be raised from other sources like the floatation of shares, issuing of bonds and debentures, past savings as well as friends and relatives.

Chapter two provides a theoretical or conceptual framework by discussing the theory of property rights. Property rights are explained as rights of ownership and refer to the legal and social relations among people in a society with respect to ownership of property. Ownership thus defines claim rights, privileges and powers the owner of the property has as well as the duties such ownership imposes on him/her as the owner and other members of the society in relation to the property. Full ownership corresponds to ownership of a bundle of 12 different rights. Two main forms of property rights exist – public rights (rights that are exercised by all members of the community or public) and private rights (an assignment of exclusive authority or rights to an individual to the use of property deemed to be his/her private property).

The origin of property rights has also been discussed in this chapter. Two philosophical theories are often used to explicate how property rights have originated, which are first occupancy and labour theories collectively, referred to as the natural rights theory. The economic importance of property rights has been identified to be internalisation of externalities and allocation of scarce resources. The philosophical theories on the origin of property rights discussed in this chapter are then applied in practical terms by using them to explain the origins of, and development of landed property rights among various ethnic groups in SSA often referred to as traditional landed property rights or ownership. The final part of the chapter looks at the misconceptions about the traditional systems of landed property ownership and an assessment of the systems shows that their operation in practice has completely been misunderstood by most foreign anthropologists, colonial administrators and nationalists' ideologues.

Chapter three is devoted to an analysis of the bases for equating land registration to ownership security. The chapter commences with an explanation of what constitutes ownership security. Even though security has been variously defined, a critical examination of such definitions suggests that the bases of some of the definitions are fundamentally flawed. Consequently in this book one appropriate definition is adopted - the degree of certainty that a person's rights will be recognized by law and, especially, by members of the society and protected when there are challenges to such rights. Land registration systems that exist globally and their differences are explained before critically analysing the bases of equating registration to security. It is established that although landed property and its registration play a critical role in the development of any nation, such a role has been grossly misunderstood. Land registration is thus made to play the wrong role when it is argued that it guarantees ownership security. It is therefore not astounding that land registration appears not to be achieving the desired objective - obviously, if the success of land registration is measured in terms of a role that it cannot play, it would appear not to be achieving its objective.

The right role of land registration is identified and explained as simply a recording keeping system that creates real estate ownership database. Such a database serves various important purposes in the economies of countries including the facilitation of property transactions like conveyancing, title searches, and taxation thereby reducing transaction costs. The actual factors that determine ownership security have been identified as: (a) societal and legal recognition of real estate ownership; (b) availability of real estate ownership dispute resolution and enforcement institutions; (c) clear demarcation of land boundaries; and (d) real estate ownership insurance. Landed property ownership needs to be secure first before registration and not the other way round as argued in the literature; that is, to register to secure ownership. If for example, there is a dispute over a plot of land, which is an element of ownership insecurity, the dispute will have to be resolved first via appropriate dispute resolution and enforcement institutions to establish the true owner or to ensure that there is security before registration. If the dispute is not resolved, in whose name will the land title be registered?

4.2. Policy Implications

The policy implications of the preceding findings are as follows. Firstly, governments in SSA and the developing world as a whole as well as the international donor community should promote land registration based on the right and critical role that it is supposed to play as identified in this book. It should be in the interest of governments to ensure that landed property ownership is registered as the governments can for example sell that information to the public; it is therefore a source of revenue. As earlier established, historically, land taxation was the main reason for the introduction of land registration in various countries several centuries ago. The continuous promotion of land registration based on the assertion that it makes title indefeasible can be an incentive for unscrupulous people to employ whatever fraudulent means available to register other people's landed property rights in their names, which is a recipe for confusion and rather a source of insecurity as illustrated in the American case of *Eliason v. Wilborn* (1929) cited in chapter one. Also, the identified determinants of real estate ownership security should inform policy formulation and programmes aimed at securing ownership.

Secondly, to stimulate especially, agricultural investment activities in SSA, various critical factors need to be given the required priority and these include interventions by government to tackle the very basic problems that have made African agriculture highly risky, unprofitable and unattractive. Thus there is the need for governments to: (a) provide storage facilities and establish agro-processing factories that will ensure that ready markets are available, which would prevent price fluctuations; (b) establish specialised financial institutions that are tailored to the needs of farmers or provide direct funding for the agricultural sector since most commercial banks normally do not want to become farmers and therefore are reluctant to provide capital for the sector - where these institutions already exist, their activities should be more focused on supporting farmers financially since, they tend not to give their core business the required attention and rather operate like other commercial banks; and (c) provide the necessary socio-economic infrastructure like good transportation net work that links the rural communities to marking centres as well as irrigation facilities for rural communities where most farming activities take place. Landed property ownership security or land registration alone cannot be the panacea to the numerous problems confronting farmers in SSA as it cannot guarantee agricultural investment and indeed, any other investment activity. International donor community support is also needed to supplement the support to be offered by national governments.

Every type of investment is determined by various factors, the overarching factor being ability to invest, which is also mainly determined by financial capability. A person's landed property ownership can be registered but if that person does not have the financial capability in the estimation of the potential mortgagee, the loan will not be granted. Other determinants include an enabling investment climate like suitable economic environment, appropriate and desirable political atmosphere, and easy access to information. Obviously, regarding easy accessibility to information, a reliable recording keeping system and for that matter land registration can facilitate activities or transactions; for example, a landed property ownership database will make it easy for property owners to be identified or verified where an investor has to acquire landed property thereby reducing transactions costs. It is, however, important to note that in this case land registration plays a facilitating role since property owners can still be identified in the absence of a landed property ownership database as earlier explained, though at a higher transaction cost.

Even if for the sake of argument it is assumed that in the absence of a land registration system, landed property owners cannot be indentified (which is not true anyway), land registration will only constitute one of the determinants of investment. In the light of this the question to ask is if the occurrence of an event is dependent on two or more factors, does it make any sense to focus on one of the factors and argue as if the occurrence of the event is contingent upon only that one factor? Certainly not as noted above! And by easily knowing who owns what landed property via the existence of a landed property ownership database alone make investment to happen? Certainly not! However, that is exactly the argument about land registration and investment!

Obviously, investment can happen if the investor has the financial capability without land registration. However there is no way investment can happen without financial capability in an environment where there is a comprehensive land registration system and landed property owners can easily be indentified or verified. It is therefore surprising that the focus is on land registration without any consideration of the rather critical and indispensable factors that actually make investment to happen. If a record keeping system like land registration could be the solution to poverty as it is argued, then there would not have been poverty in any country by now as it would have been a simple matter of registering every landed property and poverty will be completely eradicated. Even in advanced countries where there are comprehensive land registration systems, there is still poverty – there are citizens who are poor and depend on benefits from the state. Thus the promotion of land registration as the panacea to the problem of poverty amounts to a wrong prescription for the wrong malady. Such a prescription simply implies that the international donor community and governments in the developing world do not have a clear idea as to how to reduce poverty and achieve development.

REFERENCES

Abbott, D. (2005). *Encyclopaedia of Real Estate Terms*. London: Delta Alpha Publishing.

Abdulai, R. T. (2010). *Traditional Land holding Institutions in sub-Saharan Africa: The Operation of Traditional Landholding Institutions in Sub-Saharan Africa: A Case Study of Ghana*. Saarbrucken: Lambert Academic Publishing AG & Co. KG.

Abdulai, R. T. and Hammond, F. N. (2010). Landed Property Market Information Management and Access to Finance. *Property Management.* 28(3/4), 228-244.

Abdulai, R. T. and Ndekugri, I. E. (2008) Indigenous Landholding Institutions as an Impediment to Economic Use of Land: Case Studies of Tamale and Bolgatanga in Ghana. In R. A. Simons, R. M. Malmgren, and G. Small (eds.) *Research Issues in Real Estate: Indigenous Peoples and Real Estate Valuation* (pp.19-37). New York: Springer Science + Business Media, LLC,

Abdulai, R. T. and Ndekugri, I. E. (2007) Customary Landholding Institutions and Housing Development in Ghana: Case Studies of Kumasi and Wa. *Habitat International,* 31(2), 257-267.

Abdulai, R. T., Ndekugri, I. E., Olomolaiye, P. O. and Proverbs, D. G. (2007). Land Registration and security of land tenure: Case studies of Kumasi, Tamale, Bolgatanga and Wa in Ghana. *International Development Planning Review,* 29(4), 475-502.

Abdulai, R. T. and Antwi, A. (2005). Traditional landholding institutions and individual ownership of land rights in sub-Saharan Africa. *World Review of Science, Technology and Sustainable Development,* 2(3/4), 302-319

Acquaye, E. (1984). Principles and Issues. In E. Acquaye and R. Crocombe (Eds.) *Land Tenure and Rural Productivity in the Pacific Islands* (pp. 11-25). Rome: FAO.

Adams, M., Cousins, B., Manona S. (1999). Land Tenure and Economic Development in Rural South Africa: Constraints and Opportunities, Overseas Development Institute, Working Paper 125 London.

Adams, M., Sibanda, S. and Turner, S. (2000) Land tenure reform and rural livelihoods in Southern Africa. In Toulmin, C. A. and Quan, J. (Eds.) *Evolving Land Rights, Policy and Tenure in Africa* (pp.135-149). London: DFID/IIED/NRI.

Agbosu, L. K. (1990). Land Registration in Ghana: past present and the future. *Journal of Property Law*, 34, 104-127.

Alchian, A. A. (1965). Some Economics of Property Rights. *II Politic*, 30, 819-829.

Allanic, B. (2003). La nouvelle coutume urbaine: Evolution compare des filieres coutumieres de la gestion fonciere urbaine dans les pays d'Afrique subSaharienne. Le cas de Mandela Village, South Africa, ISTED, DFID.

Andre, C. and Platteau, P. (1998). Land Relations under Unbearable Stress: Rwanda caught in Malthusian Trap. *Journal of Economic Behaviour and Organization*, 34, 1-47.

Angel, S., Brown, E. Dimitrova, D. Ehrenberg, D., Heyes, J., Kusek, P., Marchesi, G., Orozco, V. Smith, L. and Ernesto, V. (2006). Secure tenure in Latin America and the Caribbean: Regularization of informal urban settlements in Peru, Mexico and Brazil. Woodrow Wilson School of Public and International Affairs, Princeton University.

Asante, S. K. B. (1975). *Property Law and Social Goals in Ghana 1844-1966.* Accra: Ghana University Press.

Asiama, S. O. (2000). Land Management in Kumasi- An overview. In S. O. Asiama (ed.) *Land Title Registration as an Effective Tool of Land Delivery and Administration,* Report of a Seminar, Centre for National Culture, Kumasi, 16th – 17th February.

Arrunada, B. A. (2001). A Global Perspective on Title Insurance. *Housing Finance International,* 16(2), 3-11.

Antwi, A. Y. (2000). Urban Land Markets in sub-Saharan Africa: A Quantitative Study of Accra, Ghana, Unpublished PhD Thesis, Napier University.

Atwood, D. A. (1990). Land Registration in Africa: The Impact on Agricultural Production. *World Development*, 18(5), 659-671.

Asante, S. K. B. (1975). *Property Law and Social Goals in Ghana*. Accra: Ghana University Press.

Barrows, R. and Roth, M. (1990). Land Tenure and Investment in African Agriculture: Theory and Evidence. *The Journal of Modern African Studies,* 28, 265-297.

Bassett, T. and Crummey, D. (Eds.) (1993). *Land in African Agrarian Systems.* Madison: The University of Wisconsin Press.

Becker, L. C. (1977). *Property Rights: Philosophic Foundations*. London: Henley and Boston Routledge.

Bell, K. C. (2006). World Bank Support for Land Administration and Management: Responding to the Challenges of the Millennium Development Goals, Paper presented at the 23rd FIG Congress, Munich, October 8-13.

Benerjee, B. (2002). Background Note, prepared for the design of Kolkata Urban Services for the Poor Project, DFID Mimeo.

Besley, T. (1995). Property Rights and Investment Incentives: Theory and Evidence from Ghana. *Journal of Political Economy,* 103, 903-937.

Bloch, P. (2003). Economic Impact of Land Policy in the English Speaking Caribbean. In A. Williams (Ed.) *Land in the Caribbean: Issues of Policy, Administration and Management in the English Speaking Caribbean* (pp. 13-30). Madison, WI: Land Tenure Centre, University of Wisconsin-Madison.

Brasselle, A., Gaspart, F., Platteau, J. (2001). Land Tenure Security and Investment Incentives: Puzzling Evidence from Burkina Faso, Centre De Recherche En Economie Du Dévelopement (Cred), Faculty of Economics, University of Namur, Rempart De La Vierge, 8, B-5000 Namur, Belgium.

Boserup, E. (1965). *The Conditions of Agricultural Growth: The Economics of Agrarian Change under Population Pressure*. Chicago: Aldine and London: Allen & Unwin.

Breman, H., Rob Groot, J. J. and Van Keulen, H. (2001). Resource limitations in Sahelian agriculture. *Global Environmental Change*, 11, 59-68.

Bromley, D. W. (2008). Formalising Property Relations in the Developing World: The Wrong Prescription for the Wrong Malady. *Land Use Policy*, 26(1), 20-27.

Bromley, D. W. (1991). *Environment and Economy.* Oxford: Blackwell.

Bruce, J. (1986). Land tenure issues in project design and strategies for agricultural development in Sub-Saharan Africa, Land Tenure Centre Paper, 128. Madison: University of Wisconsin Press.

Bruce, J. W. (1998). Review of Tenure Terminology. Tenure Brief. No. 1, WI: Land Tenure Centre, University of Wisconsin-Madison.

Buchanan, J. M. (1975). *The Limits of Liberty Between Anarchy and Leviathan.* Chicago/London: University of Chicago Press.

Buckley, R. M. and Kalarickal, J. (2006). Land Market Issues: The Mystery of Capital Revisited, Urban Land Policy – Is titling the answer? In M. Buckley and J. R. Kalarickal (eds.) *Thirty years of World Bank Shelter Lending: Directions in Development Infrastructure*, Washington DC: World Bank.

Bullard, R. and Waters, H. (1996). Land Tenure, the Root of Landownership Conflicts in Southern Africa, Past, Present and Future, Proceedings of Rural Practice Research Conference of the Royal Institution of Chartered Surveyors, London.

Cadastral Template (2003). A Worldwide Comparison of Cadastral Systems, Established under UN mandate by Resolution 4 of the 16th UNRCC-AP in Okinawa, Japan [E-text type]. www.cadastraltemplate.org

Calder, J. C., Compton, S. H, and Stein, J. (2004). A report on Title Insurance in International Real Estate Transactions. *Briefings in Real Estate Finance*, 4(2), 165-172.

Carter, M. R., Fletschner, D., and Olinto, P. (1997). Do The Poor but Efficient Survive in The Land Market? Capital Access and Land Accumulation in an Inegalitarian Agrarian Economy, Department of Agriculture and Applied Economics, University of Wisconsin, Madison.

Carter, M. R. and Wiebe, K. (1990). Access to Capital and its Impact on Agrarian Structure and Productivity in Kenya, *American Journal of Agricultural Economics,* 72(11), 46-50.

Carter, M. and Olinto, P. (2003). Getting Institutions Right for Whom? Credit Constraints and the Impact of Property Rights on the Quality and Composition of Investment, *American Journal of Agricultural Economics*, 85, 173-86.

Clay County Recorder (2004). *Torrens* [E-text type]. www.co.clay.mn.us/Depts/Recorder/RecTorr.htm

Coase, R. H. (1960). The Problem of Social Cost. *Law and Economics*, 3, 1-44.

Collier, P. and Hoeffler, A. (1998). On the Economic Causes of Civil War, Oxford Economic Papers, No. 50.

Conroy, C. Rai, A., Singh, N. and Chan, M. (1998). Conflicts Affecting Participatory Forest Management: Some Experiences from Orissa, Natural Resources Institute, Chatham.

Cotula, L., Toulmin, C. and Quan, J. (2006). Policies and Practices for Securing and Improving Access to Land. Paper presented at the 18th International Federation of Surveyors (FIG) Congress, 8-13 October, Munich.

Currie, J. M. (1981). *The Economic Theory of Agricultural Land Tenure.* Cambridge: Cambridge University Press.

Dale, P. and McLaughlin, J. D. (1989). *Land Information Management: An Introduction with Special Reference to Cadastral Problems in Third World Countries.* Oxford: Clarendon Press.

Dark, K. (2000) *Britain and the End of the Roman Empire.* London: Tempus – Publisher.

De Alessi, L. and Staaf, R. J. (1989). Property Rights and Choice. *Journal of Law and Economics,* 3, 175-200.

De Janvry, A., Platteau, J-P., Gordillo, G. and Sadoulet, E. (2001). Access to Land Policy Reforms. In A. de Janvry, G. Gordillo, J-P. Platteau, and E. Sadoulet (Eds.) *Access to Land Rural Poverty and Public Action* (pp. 1-26). Oxford: Oxford University Press.

De Soto, H. (2000). *The Mystery of Capital: Why Capitalism Triumphs in the West and fails everywhere else.* London: Bantam Press.

De Souza, F. A. M. (2001). Perceived Security of Land Tenure in Recife, Brazil. *Habitat International,* 25, 175-190.

Deininger, K. (2003). Land Policies for Growth and Poverty Reduction. World Bank Policy Research Report. World Bank, Washington DC.

Deininger, K. and Feder, G. (2001). Land Policy in developing countries. Development Note 3, World Bank, Washington DC.

Deininger, K. and Castagnini, R. (2002). Incidents and Impact of Land Conflict in Uganda, Discussion Paper, World Bank, Washington DC.

Deininger, K. (1998). The Evolution of the World Bank's Policy, World Bank mimeo, Washington DC.

Deininger, K. and Chamorro, J. S. (2002). Investment and Income Effects of Land Regularisation: The Case of Nicaragua, Development Research Group, Rural Development, World Bank Policy Research Working Paper 2752, Washington DC.

Delville, P. L. (2000). Harmonizing formal law and customary land rights in French-speaking West Africa. In C. A. Toulmin and J. Quan (eds.) *Evolving Land Rights, Policy and Tenure in Africa* (pp.97-121). London: DFID/IIED/NRI.

Demsetz, H. (1967). Towards a Theory of Property Rights. *American Economic Review,* 57, 347-595.

Derban, W. K., Derban, D. K., Ibrahim, G. and Rufasha, K. (2002). Microfinance for Housing for Low/Moderate – income Households in Ghana. Paper presented at a Conference on Housing and Urban Development for Low Income Groups in sub-Saharan Africa.

Dorward, A., Kydd, J., Morrison, J. and Urey, I. (2002). A Policy Agenda for Pro-Poor Agricultural Growth, Imperial College of Science, Technology and Medicine, Wye, Ashford, Kent, TN25 5AH, UK.

Downs, R. E. and Reyna, S. P. (Eds.) (1988). *Land and Society in Contemporary Africa*. Hanover: University of New Hampshire and London: University Press of New England.

Durand-Lasserve, A. and Payne, G. (2006). Evaluating the Impacts of Urban Land Titling: Results and Implications: Preliminary Findings, Draft Report prepared for Geoffrey Payne and Associates, London.

Durand-Lasserve, A. and Royston, L. (2000) *Holding Their ground: Secure Land Tenure for the Urban Poor in Developing Countries*. London: Earthscan Publications.

Duxbury, N. (1996). Theorising Private Property Rights, Working Paper, Faculty of Law, University of Manchester.

Elias, T. O. (1956). *The Nature of African Customary Law*. Manchester: Manchester University Press.

Enemark, S. (2005) A Cadastral Tale. Week on Geomatics, Bogota - Colombia, 8 – 13August.

Ensminger, J. (1997). Changing property rights: reconciling formal and informal rights to land in Africa. In J. N. Drobak and J. V. C. Nye (eds.) *The Frontiers of the New Institutional Economics*. London: Academic Press, London.

Famoriyo, S. (1979). Land Tenure and Agricultural Development in Nigeria, NISER, University of Ibadan, Nigeria.

Farah, I. (2004). Land Tenure and Conflict in Somalia, Summary Report of Conference on Land Tenure and Conflict in Africa: Prevention, Mitigation and Reconstruction, 9th – 10th December, Nairobi, African Centre for Technology Studies Press.

Farvacque, C. and McAuslan, P. (1992). Reforming Urban Land Policies and Institution in Developing Countries. Urban Management Program Policy Paper No. 5.

Feder, G. and Nishio, A. (1998). The Benefits of Land Registration and Titling: Economic and Social Perspectives. *Land Use Policy*, 15, 25-43.

Feeder, G. and Noronha, R. (1987). Land Rights and Agricultural Development in Sub-Saharan Africa. *Research Observer,* 2 (2), 143-169.

Feder, G. T., Onchan, Y., Chalamwong and Hangladoran, C. (1986). *Land Policies and Farm Productivity in Thailand*. Baltimore: MD John Hopkins University Press.

Fernandes, E. (2002). The Influence of de Soto's "The Mystery of Capital" *Land Lines: Newsletter of the Lincoln Institute of Land Policy,* 14(1), 5-8.

Firmin-Sellers, K. and Sellers, P. (1999). Expected Failures and Expected Successes of Land Titling in Africa. *World Development,* 27(7), 115-128.

Fiadzigbey, M. (2000). The Impact of Title Registration on Stool Land Administration. In Asiama S. O. (ed.) *Land Title Registration as an Effective Tool of Land Delivery and Administration*, Report of a Seminar, Centre for National Culture, Kumasi, 16th – 17th February.

Fisher, R. (1993). Tensions and tenures in post-apartheid South Africa. Paper presented at a Conference on International Land Tenure organized by the Royal Institution of Surveyors (RICS) and the University of East London, December 10–14, UK.

Fitzpatrick, D. (2005). Best Practice Options for the Legal Recognition of Customary Tenure. *Development and Change*, 36(3), 449-475.

Food and Agriculture Organisation (FAO) 2005. Access to Rural Land and Land Administration after Violent Conflicts. FAO Land Tenure Studies, No. 8, Rome.

Ford, D. A. (1982). Title Assurance and Settlement Charges. *Journal of the American Real Estate and Urban Economics Association*, 10(3), 297-330.

Gilbert, A. G. (2002). On the Mystery of Capital and the myths of Hernando de Soto: what difference does legal title make? *International Development Planning Review*, 24(1), 1-20.

Green, J. K. (1987). Evaluating the impact of consolidation of holdings, individualisations of tenure and registration of title: Lessons from Kenya. Land Tenure Centre Paper 129, University of Wisconsin, Madison.

Grifth-Charles, C. (2004). The Impact of Land Titling on Land Transaction Activity and Registration System Sustainability: A Case Study of St Lucia, University of Florida.

Gravois, J. (2005). The de Soto Delusion [E-text type]. http.//www.slate.com/Default.aspx?id=211792.

Galiani, S. and Shargrodsky, S. (2004). Effects of land titling on child health. *Economics and Human Biology*, 2, 353-372.

Galiani, S. and Shargrodsky, S. (2005). Property rights for the poor: Effects of land titling, Working Paper No. 29, Stanford Centre for International Development, Stanford University.

Ghana News Agency (GNA) (2011) US to Assist Smallholders' Farmers to Escape Poverty [E-text type]. http://news.myjoyonline.com/news/201106/67340.asp.

Gillingham, J. (1993). The early middle ages. In K. O. Morgan (ed.) *The History of Britain.* Oxford: Oxford University Press.

Gyekye, K. (1998). *African Cultural Values: An Introduction.* Accra: Sankofa Publishing Company Ghana.

Hallowel, A. I. (1943). The Nature and Foundation of Property Rights as a Social Institution. *Journal of Legal and Political Sociology*, 115-138.

Hardin, G. (1968). The tragedy of the Commons. *American Association for the Advancement of Science*, 162, 1243-1248.

Harvie, C. (1993). Revolution and the Rule of Law. In K. O. Morgan (ed.) *The Oxford Popular History of Britain*. Oxford: Oxford University Press.

Henssen, J. (1995). Basic principles of the main cadastral systems in the world, In: Modern Cadastres and Cadastral Innovations, Proceedings of the One Day Seminar in Delft on May 16, FIG Commission 7 and University of Melbourne, pp. 5-12.

Her Majesty (HM) Land Registry (2011). Know where you stand – register your land [E-text type] http://www1.landregistry.gov.uk/register_dev/fholdcovertable/

Herskovits, M. J. (1962). *The Human Factor on Changing Africa.* London: Routledge and Kegan Paul.

Hill, A. (1963). *The Migrant Cocoa Farmers of Southern Ghana,* Accra: University of Ghana Press Ltd.

Hobbes, T. (1951). *Leviathan.* New York: Collier.

Hogg J. E. (1920). *Registration of title to land throughout the empire : a treatise on the Law relating to warranty of title to land by registration and transactions with registered land in Australia, New Zealand, Canada, England, Ireland, West Indies, Malaya & C. A sequel to "The Australian Torrens system"* Toronto: The Carswell Company Ltd.

Hooko, D. (2000). Housing Development and Traditional Landownership in Tamale - Ghana, Unpublished PhD Thesis, University of Aberdeen.

Honoré, A. M. (1961). Ownership. In A. G. Guest (Ed.) *Oxford Essays in Jurisprudence First Series* (pp. 107-147). Oxford: Oxford Clarendon Press.

Huggins, C., Musahara, H., Mbura, K. P., Oketch, J. S. and Vlassenroot, K. (2005). Conflict in the Great Lakes Region – How is it linked with Land Registration? Paper No. 96, Natural Resource Perspectives, London, ODI.

Iliffe, J. (1995). *Africans: The History of a Continent*, Cambridge: Cambridge University Press.

Ikejiofor, C. U. Nwogu, K.C, and Nwanunobi, C. O. (2004). Informal Land Delivery Process and Access to Land for the Poor in Enugu, Nigeria, Working Paper No 2, Birmingham, School of Public Policy, University of Birmingham.

International Institute for Environment and Development (IIED) (2005). The Four Rs [E-text type]. www.policy-powertools.org/Tools/Understanding/TFR.html

International Institute for Environment and Development (IIED) (2006). Local Innovation in Securing Land Rights in Africa: Lessons from Experience, Briefing Paper, London: IIED

Jacoby, H. and Minten, B. (2005). Is Land Titling in Sub-Saharan Africa Cost Effective? Evidence from Madagascar, World Bank and Cornell University.

Janczyk, J. T. (1979). Land Title Systems, Scale of Operations, and Operating and Conversion Costs. *Journal of Legal Studies*, 8(3), 569-583.

Kagawa, A. and Turkstra, J. (2002). The process of land tenure formalisation in Peru. In G. Payne (ed) *Improving tenure security for the urban poor.* London: ITDG Publications.

Kant, P. (1887) *Philosophy of Law.* Oxford: Oxford Clarendon Press.

Kironde, L. (2006). The regulatory framework, unplanned development and urban poverty: Findings from Dar es Salaam, Tanzania. *Land Use Policy*, 460-472.

Kvitashvili, E. (200). Land and Conflict: A Toolkit for Intervention. USAID Office of Conflict Management and Mitigation, Washington DC.

Larmour, P. (2002). Policy Transfer and reversal: customary Land Registration from Africa to Melanesia. *Public Administration and Development,* 25, 151-161.

Larsson, G. (1991). *Land Registration and Cadastral Systems: Tools for Land Information and Management.* London: Longman Scientific and Technical.

Lawrance, J. C. D. (1980). Registration of Title. In J. C. D. Lawrance (ed.) *Title registration, land resource management and land use policy* (pp. 2-27). Kumasi, Land Administration Research Centre.

Li, G., Rozelle, S. and Brandt, L. (1998). Tenure, Land Rights and Farmer Investment Incentives in China. *Agricultural Economics*, 19, 63-71.

Libecap, G. D. (1989). *Contracting for Property Rights.* Cambridge: Cambridge University Press.

Lipsey, R. (1999). *Introduction to Positive Economics.* Oxford: Oxford University Press.

Locke, J. (1765). *An Essay Concerning Human Understanding in Four Books: In Three Volumes John Locke (1632-1704).* Edinburgh: Donaldson and J. Reid.

Lumumba, O. (2004). Land related conflicts in Kenya: policy and legal implications, Summary Report of Conference on Land Tenure and Conflict in Africa: Prevention, Mitigation and Reconstruction, 9th – 10th December, Nairobi, African Centre for Technology Studies Press.

Lund, C. (2008). *Local Politics and Dynamics of Property in Africa.* Cambridge: Cambridge University Press.

Mabogunje, A. L. (1990). Urban Planning and the Post-Colonial State in Africa: A Research Overview. *African Studies Review,* 33(2), 121 – 203.

MacGee, J. C. (2006). Land Titles, Credit Markets and Wealth Distributions, United Nations University/World Institute for Development Economics Research. Research Paper No. 2006/150.

MacKenzie, J-A. (2002). *Text Book on Land Law.* 9th ed. Oxford: Oxford University Press.

Mahama, C. (2008). The Mortgage Market in Ghana. In D. Ben-Shahar, C. K. Y. Leung, and S. E. Ong (Eds.) *Real Estate Issues: Mortgage Markets Worldwide* (pp. 215-230). Oxford: Blackwell Publishing.

Manaoukian, M. (1952). *Tribes in of Northern Territories of the Gold Coast.* London: International African Institute.

Mathuba, B. M. (1999). Land boards and customary land administration in Botswana. Paper presented at the DFID Workshop on Land Rights and Sustainable Development in Sub-Saharan Africa: Lessons and Ways Forward in Land Tenure Policy, Sunningdale, February 16–19, UK.

McAuslan, P. (2000). Only the name of the Country Changes: The Diaspora of 'European' Land Law in Commonwealth Africa. In C. Toulmin and J. Quan, (Eds.) *Evolving land rights, policy and tenure in Africa* (pp. 75-95). London: DFID/IIED/NRI.

Migot-Adholla, S. E., Place, F. and Oluoch-Kosura, W. (1994). Security of tenure and land productivity in Kenya. In J. W. Bruce and S. E. Migot-Adholla (Eds.) *Searching for land tenure security in Africa.* Debuque Iowa: Kendall/Hunt Publishing Company.

Migot-Adholla, S. (1999). Principles of the World Bank's land policy. Paper presented at the DFID Workshop on Land Rights and Sustainable Development in Sub-Saharan Africa: Lessons and Ways Forward in Land Tenure Policy, Sunningdale, UK.

Migot-Adholla, S., Hazell, P., Blarel, B., Place, F. (1991). Indigenous Land Rights Systems in Sub-Saharan Africa: A Constraint on Productivity? *The World Bank Economic Rev*iew, **5**(1), 155-175.

Migot-Adholla, S. (1993). *Indigenous Land Rights Systems in Sub-Saharan Africa: A Constraint on Productivity?* Oxford: Oxford University Press.

Milgrom, P. and Roberts, J. (1992). *Economics, Organization and Management*. Upper Saddle River, USA: Prentice Hall.

Moody, B. A. (2005). A Timeline for Title Insurance. *Mortgage Banking*, 65(11), 57-62.

Munzer, S. R. (1990). *A Theory of Property*. Cambridge, New York: Cambridge University Press.

Naire, K. (1984). Transforming Traditionally: Land and Labour use in Agriculture in Asia and Africa, Perspectives on Asian and African development, No. 1, Riverdale, Maryland.

Odgen, C. K. (1931). The Theory of Legislation. In C. K. Odgen (Ed.) *Jeremy Bentham* (1784) (pp.109-123). London: Routledge and Kegan Paul.

Okoin, J. R. M. (1999). Cote d'Ivoire's rural land-use plan: an innovative approach towards an appropriate rural land tenure code. Paper presented at the DFID Workshop on Land Rights and Sustainable Development in Sub-Saharan Africa: Lessons and Ways Forward in Land Tenure Policy, 16-19 February, Sunningdale, UK.

Okoth-Ogendo, H. W. O. (1982). The Perils of Land Tenure Reform. Paper presented at a workshop on Land Policy and Agricultural Production in Eastern and Southern African Countries, Gaborone, Botswana.

Ollenu, N. A. (1962). *Customary Land Law in Ghana*. London: Sweet and Maxwell.

Palmer, D. (1998). Security, Risk and Registration. *Land Use Policy*, 15(1), 83-94.

Payne, G. (1997). *Urban Land Tenure and Property Rights in Developing Countries: A Review*. London: Intermediate Technology Publications.

Payne, G. Durand-Lasserve, A. and Rakodi, C. (2009). The Limits of Land Titling and Home Ownership. *Environment and Urbanisation*, 21(2), 443–462.

Payne, G. Durand-Lasserve, A. and Rakodi, C. (2007). Urban Land Titling Programmes. In Brother, M. E. and Solberg, J-A. (Eds.) *Legal empowerment – a way out of poverty*. Norway: Norwegian Ministry of Foreign Affairs.

Pemberton, L. (1992). *HM Land Registry: An Historical Perspective.* London: HM Land Registry.

Pingali, P. L. (1989). Institutional and Environmental Constraints to Agricultural Intensification. Population and Development Review Supplement: Rural Development and Population. *Institutions and Policy,* 15, 243-260.

Platteau, J. P. (1996). Physical Infrastructure as a Constraint on Agricultural Growth: The Case of Sub-Saharan Africa. *Oxford Development Studies*, 24(3), 189-219.

Plucknett, T. F. T. (2007). *A Concise History of the Common Law*. 5th Ed. New Jersey: Lawbook Exchange Ltd. Union.

Posner, R. A. (1981). *Economic Analysis of Law*. 2nd ed. Chicago: Little Brown.

Pound, R. (1954). *An Introduction to the Philosophy of Law.* Oxford: Oxford Clarendon Press.

Powelson, J. P., and Stock, R. (1990). The Peasant Betrayed, The CATO Institute, Washington DC.

Quan, J. (2000). Land Tenure, Economic Growth and Poverty in sub-Saharan Africa. In J. Quan and C. Toulmin (Eds.) *Evolving Land Rights, Policy and Tenure in Africa* (pp. 31-50) London: DFID/IIED/NRI.

Rattray, R. S. (1923). *Ashanti Law and Constitution.* Accra: Ghana Publishing Corporation.

Raynaut, C. (1976). Transformation du système de production et inégalité économique: le cas d'un village Haoussa. *Canadian Journal of African Studies,* 10, 279-306.

Richard, P. (2003). Controversy over Recent West African Wars: An Agrarian Question, Unpublished Notes for an ISS Seminar, 6th October, ISS, The Hague.

Riddall, J. G. (2003). *Land Law*. 7th ed. London: LexisNexis.

Ramirez, C. Daniel, G. and Riofrio, G. (2005). Land Titling a Path to Urban Inclusion? Policy and Practice of the Peruvian Model. Paper presented at the N-AERUS Conference, Barcelona, Spain.

Roth, M. and Haase, D. (1998). Land Tenure Security and Agricultural Performance in Southern Africa, Land Tenure Centre Paper, University of Wisconsin-Madison, Madison.

Schlager, E. and Ostrom, E. (1992). Property-Rights Regimes and Natural Resources: a Conceptual Analysis. *Land Economics*, 68, 249-62.

Scott, R. (1984). The Multipurpose Land Information System in the Public Sector Community of North American Continent, FIG Congress, Montreux.

Simpson, S. R. (1984). *Land Law and Registration*. London: Surveyor's Publications.

Simpson, S. R. (1976). *Land Law and Registration*. Cambridge: Cambridge University Press.

Sims, D. (2002). What is Secure Tenure in Egypt? In G. Payne (Ed.) *Land Rights and Innovation: Improving Tenure Security for the Urban Poor* (pp. 79-99). London: ITDG.

Sirmans, G. S. and Dumm, R. E. (2006). Title Insurance: An Historical Perspective. *Journal of Real Estate Literature*, 14(3), 293-320.

Sjaastad, E. and Bromley, D. W. (1997). Indigenous Land Rights in Sub-Saharan Africa, Appropriation, Security and Investment Dynamics. *World Development,* 25(4), 549-62.

Sjaastad, E. and Bromley, D. W. (2000). The Prejudices of Property Rights: On Individualism, Specificity and Security in Property Regimes. *Development Policy Review*, 18, 365-389.

Stamm, V. (2000). Land tenure policy: an innovative approach from Cote d' Ivoire. DryLands Issue Paper 91, IIED, London.

Sukumaran, K. (1999). Hunted, hounded, and homeless in Indore: A Report of large scale forced evictions, IPT Report, India.

Taylor, J. (1988). The ethical foundations of the market. In V. Ostrom, et al. (Eds.) *Rethinking Institutional Analysis and Development: Issues, Alternatives and Choices*. San Francisco: California Institute for Contemporary Studies Press.

Thirtle, C. Lin, L. and Jenifer P. (2003). The Impact of Research-Led Agricultural Productivity Growth on Poverty Reduction in Africa, Asia and Latin America. *World Development*, 31(12), 1959–1975.

Thompson, M. P. (2003). *Modern Land Law*. 2nd ed., Oxford: Oxford University Press.

Toulmin, C. (2008). Securing land and property rights in sub-Saharan Africa: The role of local institutions. *Land Use Policy,* 26, 10-19.

Toulmin, C. and Longbottom, J. (2001). West African Land: Rights, Poverty and Growth. IIED Drylands Programme, Edinburgh, UK.

Toulmin, C. and Quan, J. (2000). Evolving land rights, tenure and policy in Sub-Saharan Africa. In J. Quan and C. Toulmin (eds.) *Evolving Land Rights, Policy and Tenure in Africa* (pp.207-228). London: DFID/IIED/NRI.

Törhönen, M. (2004). Sustainable Land Tenure And Land Registration In Developing Countries, Including A Historical Comparison With An Industrialised Country, Computers, Environment and Urban Systems.

United States Agency for International Development (USAID) (2005). *Land and Conflict: A Toolkit for Intervention*. Washington DC, USA: USAID.

United Nations Centre for Human Settlements (UNCHS) (1999). *The Global Campaign for Secure Tenure*, United Nations, Geneva.

Varley, A. (1987). The relationship between tenure legalisation and housing improvements: Evidence from Mexico. *Development and Change,* 18, 463-481.

Wannasai, N. and Shrestha R. P. (2007). Role of Land Tenure Security and Farm Household Characteristics on Land Use Change in the Prasae Watershed, Thailand, *Land Use Policy*, 25, 214–224.

West, H. W. (2000). On African Land Holding: A Review of Tenurial Change and Land Policies in Anglophone Africa. Lewiston: Edwin Millen.

White, C. M. N. (1959). A Survey of African Land Tenure in Northern Rhodesia. *Journal of African Administration*, 11 (4), 171-188.

Woodman, G.R. (1985). Customary law, state courts, and the notion on institutionalization of norms in Ghana and Nigeria. In A. Allot and G. R. Woodman (eds.) *People's Law and State Law: The Bellagio Papers*. Dordrecht: Foris.

Woodman, G. (1986). Land Title Registration without prejudice: the Ghana land title registration law 1986. *Journal of African Law*, 31, 119-135.

Woodman, G. R. (1996). *Customary Land Law in the Ghanaian Courts*. Accra: Ghana Universities Press.

World Bank (2005). *Doing business in 2005: Removing obstacles to Growth*. Oxford: Oxford University Press.

World Bank (2006). Afghanistan Urban Land Policy Notes, Series 5.2. World Bank, Washington DC.

World Bank (2007). World Bank Assistance to Agriculture in Sub-Saharan Africa: An IEG Review, World Bank, Washington DC.

World Bank (2010). World Bank Development Report, World Bank Washington DC.

Zevenbergen, J. (2004). A Systems Approach to Land Registration and Cadastre. *Nordic Journal of Surveying and Real Estate Research*, 1(1), 11-24.

INDEX

A

B

C

D

E

F

G

H

I

J

K

L

M

N

O

P

T

U

V

W

Y